THE GOSPEL OF

Chapters 1 – 1.

To
Edward and Anne

THE GOSPEL OF JOHN

Chapters 1 – 11

PASTORAL AND THEOLOGICAL STUDIES

including some sermons

RONALD S. WALLACE

[handwritten signature: With my best wishes? Ronald S Wallace.]

SCOTTISH ACADEMIC PRESS
EDINBURGH

Published by
Scottish Academic Press Ltd.
56 Hanover Street
Edinburgh EH2 2DX

First published 1991
ISBN 0 7073 0700 7

Printed in Great Britain by
Billing and Sons Ltd, Worcester

CONTENTS

The English translation used throughout, unless otherwise stated, is that of the Revised Standard Version.

FOREWORD

For over fifty years, ministering to various congregations, I have often preached from the Gospel of John, given it a place in my bible class teaching, studied it with fellow parish ministers, and lectured on it to lay people. I have taught it as a class subject in theological seminary. This book has been written to share with pastors and others who are concerned to study the Bible, some of the insights into the text that have come to me in the course of such a ministry.

My custom in preaching or teaching was to divide the text into sections which appeared to have some unity, and to go through it, section by section, story by story, incident by incident, concentrating mainly on the dynamic movement of the incident or the thought. Through this procedure I tried to bring out the meaning of words and sentences and thus the important theological or practical lessons which might help my hearers to see what I saw, and to hear what I myself had already heard as I worked with each passage.

As a pastor I was always chiefly concerned to find what the Spirit is saying to the Church today through the text as we have it before us. I often felt in my ministry that I discovered the meaning of a passage most clearly as I found it applying itself directly to the pastoral situation which I faced among those who were to listen to me. In writing this book moreover, I have found often that I could best convey the meaning of the passage before me if I kept the rhetorical form in which its meaning came to me in the course of my work. The reader will therefore find that while certains sections of the book reflect how I treated the passage under review in bible class studies or lectures, more often the comments indicate what I said in the pulpit, and sometimes take the form of a sermon.

Some time ago I attended a seminar for post-graduate students led by a visiting scholar of international reputation. The passage under discussion was the ministry of the Baptist as it is related in the first chapter of John. Some new background material of which I had not been fully aware was brought to light, and an interpretation was given which raised questions in my mind as to whether the approach I had previously made to the passage was justifiable. A student present, however, remarked that from these and other studies he had engaged in, he had come to wonder whether anyone today, having listened to such background revelations about John's Gospel, could now really preach from it at all. In reply the lecturer graciously conceded, however, that a preacher could legitimately take liberties with the text which were not open to himself as a scholar. Such a reply emboldened me to decide not to alter what I had already written on John, chapter I. Indeed, I was relieved to feel that there might be a place, even on the shelves of a serious New Testament student's library, for a book showing how a preacher took this liberty allowed to him in his task.

Only here and there in the book have I been able to acknowledge my indebtedness to the many commentaries, academic essays, and sermons I have read on the Gospel, over the years. (I have lost all the other references I may have had.) Of course I read everything I could, and latterly I lived near a well-stocked theological library. I liked Hoskyn's commentary best of all, and I must record my admiration for Raymond Brown's more recent work.

My dear wife was my closest companion and collaborator throughout the whole ministry during which this book took shape. She was nearly always there when I preached, and often when I taught. Up till now she always read, and improved what I wrote. I have not felt I wanted to consult anyone in her place. This is why there may be infelicities in the text, and things said which her acute mind would have corrected. I have to thank Dr Douglas Grant, for the encouragement he has given me to produce this volume, and I am grateful to Rev Dr. R. B. W. Walker for careful proof-reading and helpful suggestions.

As I was preparing its final draft, I had the opportunity of preaching some of it in "series" to the congregations of Juniper Green Church, Edinburgh and St Paul's, Galashiels. It encouraged me that my hearers were so warmly appreciative. Then I was invited to go to Talladega, Alabama, for three months during the winter of 1988 – 89 to teach John's

Gospel to the 'Caravan Bible Class'. I am most grateful for their warm hospitality and friendship, and for the extraordinary helpful and inspiring opportunity it gave me to teach such a large, eager and intelligent gathering of adults while I was preparing the book.

Of course in preaching and teaching I have become aware of the assumptions I have had to make about the purpose and authority of the 'writer' of the Gospel. For the sake of the reader I have occasionally given in the text a reason for the interpretation I have made (see e.g. pp19ff. and 106f.) and I have clarified the presuppositions of my own personal approach in an introductory article.

Edinburgh, September 1990

INTRODUCTION

An Approach to the Gospel

H.R. MACKINTOSH, teaching us theology in the early 1930's, advised us, in facing the doubts and problems we might have, to "get into the presence of Jesus" and to allow him to make God's own presence and power real to us. He was appealing to us to turn to the Gospel accounts of Jesus, and to read them with devoted and receptive minds.

Mackintosh believed that the Gospels were there to give us access to the living Christ today, and to enable us to enter a fellowship with him no less influential than that enjoyed by the Apostles themselves, and many other contemporaries, in his earthly presence. Such fellowship with Jesus in the days of his flesh inevitably brought the early disciples to a profound experience of repentance, accompanied by the immediate and complete assurance that their sins were forgiven. It was Mackintosh's concern that by our own recourse to the Gospel story we ourselves should first of all experience in some way the forgiving love of Christ.

He was confident, moreover, that the forgiving love thus experienced would help to confirm our faith in the divinity of Jesus himself, justify to our minds the authority that rings through all his teaching about God and life, and bring our lives under the constraint of his call to surrender our self-will and to follow him, even laying down our lives for his sake. A continuing openness to his influence would indeed ultimately lead us to give him the highest place in the universe. The logic of the experience would be inescapable: "only God can forgive, yet Jesus has forgiven us, only God has a right to demand the complete sacrifice of another for his own sake, yet the Jesus we know and hear through the Gospels makes such a demand upon us!" We must immediately confess that he is Lord, and cannot doubt that since he has enabled us to overcome sin, he has the power to see through every other difficulty which life, either in this world or beyond, can put in our way.

Of course Mackintosh in his theology also took us to the heart of every important aspect of the teaching of the Pauline Epistles. He directed our thought, faith and devotion to the exalted Christ. He gave us a full understanding of the meaning of the Cross as it developed in the thought of the growing Church. Nevertheless, like Luther and Calvin he always saw the seeds of such a fuller development of the faith already there in what the earliest disciples experienced, apprehended, and began to understand when they were with him in the flesh. Moreover, like the Reformers he always stressed our need to return again and again to the One presented to us in the Gospels, in order to maintain our grasp of the faith in its fullness.

In our New Testament studies at the time I am referring to, the Gospel of John was sometimes set apart from the other "synoptic" accounts as being of lesser historical value. Matthew, Mark and Luke alone were accepted as intended to present us with reliable historical information about the human Jesus as he was actually seen and experienced by his disciples in "the days of his flesh". The Gospel of John, however, was regarded as a carefully drawn picture of the God-man as he was seen within the faith of the early church by a writer who was concerned not to relate historical fact, but rather to give us a "spiritual" Gospel. It was also held that its writer, in the picture he gave us of Jesus, was especially concerned to relate his person, work, and teaching to those who belonged to the contemporary Greek world of culture and thought.

It seems important, however, that in our modern "quest for the historical Jesus" we should not in any way neglect the fourth Gospel. I myself have come to think of it as written under the guidance and close supervision of the Apostle John. He knew the tradition circulated through the other Gospels. He did not wish to repeat this in his own Gospel though he confirmed it where he could. He had, however, other things to say than had been already said. He himself had been differently impressed than were his fellow Apostles by some of the events which had taken place, and had been more sensitive to certain aspects of the person, teaching, and life-work of Jesus when he had been with them. It was his mission to give this witness in his own independent way in the midst of the circumstances surrounding him.

While all the Gospel accounts of Jesus continually stress his real humanity and his close identification with us in our human weakness and need, a fuller picture is given in John's Gospel than in the others of the difference, indeed of the apartness, between himself and us. We find in the fourth Gospel much that isolates him from us, and exalts him in character far above anything that can normally be defined as "human". His personal sinlessness and holiness seem to put him at a distance from us. Moreover, even while he is so much at home with us in this world, he seems to belong to another world, one which he uniquely shares with his Father in Heaven. John obviously threw such aspects of Jesus' person into strong relief because he believed that it was important for the Church to have them in mind in its devotion and preaching. His holiness and majesty do not repel but attract us to him. In his sheer apartness he is near to our need. He is able to save us not only because he is like us, but also because he is different from us. The isolation into which he was "lifted up" not only on his cross but also even in his exaltation draws us to himself (John 12: 32).

We need not imagine that John's presentation of Jesus is in any way an artificially drawn portrait designed to emphasise a theological point. His account is what he remembered from his fellowship with the Lord. That a Gospel was given its final form even many years after the occurrence of the events it relates need not imply that its witness is any less reliable, historically or otherwise, than any writing more immediately composed. We suggest that John was able to penetrate the history which he remembered and probe its meaning all the more accurately, because of the greater historical distance between himself and the events which it was his purpose to relate. On such late reflection, under the influence of the Spirit, he was possibly able to see what had really been there when his mind was not so acute and sensitive to the realities which Jesus presented to those around him through the years of his early ministry. We can well imagine, moreover, that as the years passed it would become impossible for the Apostle to distinguish between what had been there in the earlier layers of memory and what came to clarification through later reflection and insight.

I have found helpful the suggestion that there was a Johannine circle of disciples who were active in preaching and teaching the Gospel under the Apostle's leadership. Such preaching involved the continual re-telling and re-consideration of the incidents and stories within the presentation of the whole proclamation and its purpose would be to open to the hearer the same possibilities of seeing the glory of the "Word made flesh", and of receiving "from his fullness", as had been open to the contemporaries of Jesus when he was himself living and working among them.

There is no doubt that to all the Gospel writers everything that Jesus did was full of significance. His miracles, for example, as well as being revelations of his compassionate humanity and unique demonstrations of his power, are also signs pointing to his Messiahship and revealing the place he has come to fulfil in the life of the people of God. The Apostle John, however was especially sensitive to the fact that every deed of the Word was itself uniquely and inevitably itself a Word of God. When he was with Jesus as a disciple he had found that certain events which he had been involved in, or had witnessed, had especially impressed his mind. They had clarified his vision of who Jesus was, and had deepened his understanding of what he had come to do. As he had thought over such events and spoken of them in his later ministry he had come to regard them as signs of the "glory as of the only Son from the Father" (John 1:14), that was always there in Jesus seeking expression in his activity. He believed, too, that in the ministry that he fulfilled amongst people during his earthly life Jesus was continually giving signs of the kind of ministry he was going to fulfil through his Apostles, after he sent them out to continue his work in his name. We have often discovered what we believe to have been an intended meaning in the text, when we have regarded it as bearing witness not simply to one historic event but to "Jesus Christ ... The same yesterday and today and forever" (see pp 19ff.).

For the purpose of handing on his own unique testimony in one Gospel, John selected certain of these signs and encounters which had especially impressed themselves on his mind and which he treasured in his memory. He put them within a more convincing historical framework than is found by reference only to the Synoptic Gospels. Though it is not impossible to harmonize these Gospels with that of John, it seems indeed that John was more concerned than the other writers to be "historical". Yet he also indicates the wealth of meaning which he found in much of what Jesus had done by bringing into his narrative frequent allegorical suggestions. Such allegorical elements are to be regarded not as artificially contrived, but as embedded deeply within the unique history itself. They are pointers through which he is inviting us to "see through a glass darkly" into the Kingdom of God which has been brought into our midst in Jesus.

Though he had such concern to bear faithful testimony to the "Word ... made flesh", John made no attempt to reproduce for us many of the sayings, parables and sermons with which the hearers of the other Gospels would be familiar. There was no need for this in the Church of his day. He himself may have been more sensitive however, than other disciples to certain aspects of Jesus' teaching of which they give us less clear indications than John would have wished. He had possibly in private asked questions of Jesus and discussed with him the themes on which he had such intense interest. He does not seek to cast what he remembers in a style directly recognisable by those already familiar with the other Gospels. Indeed, in John's Gospel, Jesus expresses himself in a language and style only occasionally used by him in the Synoptics, but used freely by John himself in the Epistles which he wrote later to the Churches.

We must not set too narrow limits to the language and phraseology Jesus could have used during his earthly ministry. Might he not have used the kind of language John presents to us, on sufficiently many occasions for it to take a firm grip on the minds of some of his hearers to whom he knew it was especially relevant and appealing? It may be that as the corpus of Jesus' teaching had been stored in his mind over many years, and dominated all his thought, it had both affected, and had been affected by, his own way of thinking and style of speaking, without any contamination of its own true force and meaning. It is a remarkable fact that when we are reading through the New Testament and we turn from hearing the spoken words of Jesus as they are brought to us in the Synoptic Gospels to the discourses quoted to us in John, we know ourselves still listening to his one authentic voice.

CHAPTER 1

THE PROLOGUE

John I. 1 – 18

1 In the beginning was the Word, and the Word was with God, and the Word was God. [2]He was in the beginning with God; [3]all things were made through him, and without him was not anything made that was made. [4]In him was life, and the life was the light of men. [5]The light shines in the darkness, and the darkness has not overcome it.

[6]There was a man sent from God, whose name was John. [7]He came for testimony, to bear witness to the light, that all might believe through him. [8]He was not the light, but came to bear witness to the light.

[9]The true light that enlightens every man was coming into the world. [10]He was in the world, and the world was made through him, yet the world knew him not. [11]He came to his own home, and his own people received him not. [12]But to all who received him, who believed in his name, he gave power to become children of God; [13]who were born, not of blood nor of the will of the flesh nor of the will of man, but of God.

[14]And the Word became flesh and dwelt among us, full of grace and truth; we have beheld his glory, glory as of the only Son of the Father. [15](John bore witness to him, and cried, "This was he of whom I said, 'He who comes after me ranks before me, for he was before me'.") [16]And from his fullness have we all received, grace upon grace. [17]For the law was given through Moses; grace and truth came through Jesus Christ. [18]No one has ever seen God; the only Son, who is in the bosom of the Father, he has made him known.

1

The Prologue to the Gospel reads like a hymn in praise of Christ – a doxology in which the author expresses his devotion to the One who has brought light, life and hope into a lost and perishing world. In it he gives his testimony to the glory which he saw in Jesus, and the eternal life which he received from him as he lived with him on earth. He gives us a summary of the faith and experience into which he hopes the reading of the Gospel will introduce us.

We need not spend much time in the study of the verbal detail of the prologue before we proceed to the Gospel. What it is meant to tell us is best appreciated if its contents are remembered and referred to often as we read the book itself. It is meant, indeed, to direct us to a better appreciation of the witness of the Gospel itself to Jesus. It is in this way simply a key to the understanding of what follows.

The Word and Creation

The poem before us will remind us, as we turn to the Gospel, that the Word spoken in the life, death, and resurrection of Jesus is the true and full expression of what God is, and of what he ever was, in the mystery of his own being – even before creation. God uttered himself when he uttered the Word spoken in Jesus.

Jesus brought into this world the life as well as the light of God. These two are inseparable. *In him was life, and the life was the light of men.* In seeing what he has come to reveal to us we have seen the eternal light that was there in the beginning with God. In our fellowship with him we have tasted the eternal fellowship which God from the beginning desired to share with mankind.

Moreover we have begun also to understand the meaning and purpose of creation itself, for the Word spoken in Jesus is the "Wisdom" by which God made the world, and which he expressed in its making. Here, in and through him, we find a clear answer to the questions: "Who am I, and what am I here for?" Here in Him, we are in touch with the One who holds everything in the universe together, and who alone can keep it healthy and in order till its final purpose is fulfilled.

The Word and the Darkness

The Gospel before us is the story not only of what is revealed and given in Jesus, but also of what was overcome by Jesus. It is the story of a long relentless conflict. He has come to rescue the world from bondage, and to put right what has absurdly and tragically gone wrong with it. Yet at every step of his way he is opposed. Those in charge of human affairs react to him with deadly hatred. His crucifixion at their hands is a central theme of the unfolding story. *The light shines in the darkness,* a darkness that seeks to *overcome it.* The greater and clearer the light, the more intense and forceful the darkness.

The common people around him are in the end no better than their leaders. They welcome him for a while but eventually despise and reject. Their decision is all the more absurd and tragic because they were *his own* people. They had been chosen by the Father to receive him, to prepare a place where he would find a welcome and nurture when he came. They had been trained for centuries to understand the message he would bring, the mission he would accomplish, and to give him devotion, service and honour as their Prophet, Priest and King. The appeals he made were irresistible and yet they resisted. The signs he gave them were irrefutable, and yet they argued that he was an impostor. He will offer them their liberty, they will prefer bondage.

Yet his victory was all the more complete because of their very efforts to destroy him. The humiliation to which they subjected him manifested clearly his glory. Each step they took to destroy him fulfilled the plan made by God his Father from all eternity to manifest his redeeming power and love. In lifting him up to die they set him on the throne from which he has ever since won and ruled the hearts of generations who were now to become his own.

The writer of the prologue links up the darkness which Jesus confronted among his own people in Galilee and Jerusalem with a darkness that seems to have arisen there, *"in the beginning"* when God uttered his creative Word and the world came into being. Even then the same darkness sought to overcome the same light. The Prologue thus reminds us at this point that the conflict which we will see Jesus entering when he came to earth was primordial in its origin, age-long in its implications and that his victory was cosmic in its issues and effects. The challenge which he takes up to settle once for all as he goes to Golgotha was the challenge presented by the powers of darkness to God's sovereignty and love at the very moment of creation. He has come to destroy the works of the devil. (1 John 3:8).

"The Word became flesh and dwelt among us"

This affirmation expresses the faith of his disciples as they looked back over his life with them on earth.

He was flesh as we are flesh – a truly human being with all our natural affections. They knew his mother, and his brothers. They knew that he had been trained as a carpenter. They knew he felt as they themselves felt in many of the common situations and problems that vex us all on our way through life. Under the varied circumstances of his ministry they knew how human his reactions were. They had seen his tears. They had noticed his surprise, wonder and thankfulness in success, his disappointment and frustration in failure, his tiredness under the strain of over-exertion, his occasional weariness, his sensitivity to insult. They knew that in his sheer weakness at times he had to find consolation and strength in desperate prayer. Flesh is that which, like everything human, fades and perishes with the passing of time. It is prone, they believed, to disease and death.

Yet he rose from the dead, and his resurrection confirmed and explained many other thoughts and experiences which had come to them in his fellowship. At times they had heard him pray and speak to God as if he himself were already in heaven. At times he had made pronouncements about God, life and the future as if he had a clarity of vision, fullness of understanding, and absolute certainty on matters entirely beyond the range of any human mind. To listen to him simply unfolding his own mind had been to listen to the Word and Wisdom of God. Had he not forgiven sins in his own name and on his own authority? Had he not called on people to lay down their lives for his own sake? They had themselves felt that from the moment he called them, it was eternal gain to go on with him, eternal loss to reject his way and offer. The confession made first by Thomas reflected the faith that each one of them finally came to: "My Lord and my God" (John 20:28).

Such thoughts and questions about the mystery of Jesus' personal life led to questions and thoughts about his birth. John did not need to repeat the story of the virgin birth, though there is evidence in his Gospel that he accepted the tradition. He expresses the whole matter much more briefly: *The Word became flesh and dwelt among us.* There was an incarnation. God did not merely choose this child of Mary, and condescend to express his divine character in the way he lived, and died, and triumphed. In this man, rather he gave us his own presence, "his very self and essence all-divine," dwelling "*among us*". The testimony of the whole Gospel is that while he dwelt with us in the flesh he was also no less truly dwelling with God.

"We have beheld . . . We have received . . . !"

As there was in the coming of Jesus into the world an incarnation, so also there was concealment. No one has expressed this mystery better than Charles Wesley:

> "Veiled in flesh the Godhead see;
> Hail the Incarnate Deity."

The eternal God – a babe in a manger – ruling the universe!
There are traces in the Old Testament of how God practised such concealment when he dealt with Israel, his people. We are shown how often he went to work most powerfully where there was little outward sign of his activity and how he could hide his glory when he was about to reveal it.

"Truly thou art a God who hidest Thyself O God of Israel the Saviour" wrote one of the great Prophets (Isa. 45:15). He may have been thinking of such events as the destruction of Pharoah's power in Egypt when instead of launching the battleships of a mighty enemy on the Nile, he launched a little helpless male child in an ark of bullrushes to be pitied and picked up by Pharoah's daughter.

Or he may have remembered that when God wanted to "visit" and have personal intercourse with certain people in the earlier history of Israel he chose to come and show himself present to them, in the humble form of an angel or even of a human-like visitor. We do not wonder that in such aspects of God's work in former times, our forefathers in the faith saw analogies of how he was going to set about his redeeming work in the days to come.

Another Old Testament text from the same prophet foreshadows with even more fitting detail the concealment that was to take place during the early (sometimes called "hidden") years of Jesus' life: "For he grew up before him like a young plant, and like a root out of the dry ground; he had no form or comeliness that we should look at him, and no beauty that we should desire him." (Isa. 53:2.)

The hiddenness referred to by the Prophet was sustained and complete during these early years. People around Jesus of Nazareth heard nothing from him, and saw nothing in him that could lead them towards discipleship. It was only when he began his earthly ministry declaring himself to be the Messiah that they began to hear and to see. The Baptist himself was the first to see his glory and truth, and he saw it with a clarity and fullness excelled in Jesus' lifetime by no other witness who followed him. *There was a man sent from God whose name was John. He came for testimony to bear witness to the light, that all might believe through him.*

Central to the story in John's Gospel (as in the others too) is the account of a chosen group of witnesses – the twelve. It is their testimony that is echoed in the prologue and given in the Gospel. *"We have beheld . . . We have received."* That they should have been chosen to hear and receive was to them miraculously due to the grace of God who had not only revealed himself to them in Jesus, but had given them the inward illumination and disposition to see and believe. They recognised in him what no merely human eye could see. They describe what they saw as his *glory*. They speak of what they received as a sharing of his *fullness* and they add their testimony to its abundance:*grace upon grace*. There was no end to it. This is why they preached, and why the Gospel was written. Their witness is handed down to us so that we too, reading and listening, may see, believe, and receive as they did.

The poem ends as it began, with praise. What is seen and given in Jesus puts everything else into the shade! Even the Law, which in its day brought light and life to those who loved it, is now seen to be outdated and powerless, for it demands and threatens before it gives: *The Law was given through Moses; grace and truth came through Jesus Christ.*

He sums up: *No one has ever seen God; the only Son, who is in the bosom of the Father, he has made him known.* He is not here giving the result of any careful research he had made either into the other religions of his day or into its current philosophical thought. He is simply expressing his wonder at the grace he has encountered and the glory he has seen in Jesus. What is given and seen here can be found only in Him, and nowhere else. He is giving expression also to its finality. H.R. Mackintosh put it simply and clearly for us in one of his lectures: "Never in any experience of God here or hereafter will you or I ever find anything that is not already there for us in Jesus Christ, the Word become flesh."

CHAPTER 2

THE BAPTIST UNDER QUESTIONING
John 1: 19 – 28

19 And this is the testimony of John, when the Jews sent priests and Levites from Jerusalem to ask him, "Who are you?" [20]He confessed, he did not deny, but confessed, "I am not the Christ." [21]And they asked him, "What then? Are you Eli'jah?" He said, "I am not." "Are you the prophet?" And he answered, "No." [22]They said to him then, "Who are you? Let us have an answer for those who sent us. What do you say about yourself?" [23]He said, "I am the voice of one crying in the wilderness, 'Make straight the way of the Lord,' as the prophet Isaiah said."

24 Now they had been sent from the Pharisees. [25]They asked him, "Then why are you baptizing, if you are neither the Christ, nor Eli'jah, nor the prophet?" [26]John answered them, "I baptize with water; but among you stands one whom you do not know, [27]even he who comes after me, the thong of whose sandal I am not worthy to untie." [28]This took place in Bethany beyond the Jordan, where John was baptizing.

The Last and Greatest of the Prophets

John the Baptist, in his early preaching, re-echoed the message of all the great Old Testament Prophets. He proclaimed a new and better age for the oppressed and the righteous. He spoke of a Messiah who was to usher in the Kingdom of God. He would bring blessing to those prepared to welcome him. He would baptize with the Holy Spirit. He

8

would cleanse public life. What he rejected would be consumed with unquenchable fire. His central theme was repentance. Each must forsake his sordid aims and lusts, begin to deal righteously with his neighbour, and share with the needy. The rulers of this present world must tremble. The axe was now laid to the root of every corrupt and proud tree.

The crowds who flocked to hear him compared John to men like Moses, Elijah, Isaiah and Jeremiah. At last, after 300 years of silence, they believed, God was speaking again a living prophetic word to their nation, and was about to intervene decisively in its historical destiny.

There was one striking difference between John and his predecessors. When the great prophets of Israel had spoken about the coming of the Messiah's Kingdom, their timing had been vague. They had spoken much of the "latter days" or "days to come" when most of their prophecies would find fulfilment. John's message to his generation, however, was that the "latter days" so often promised as future, were here and now. The Kingdom of God was "at hand" and ready to break into this present world in its fullness. Israel's Messiah, moreover, John declared dramatically, was present already in the world. Somewhere in their midst, at present unrecognized, God was preparing him for his life's work and soon, at the decisive great moment, his glory and his Kingdom would be revealed and discovered. John believed he had authority from God to prepare a group of representative people who themselves would search for and serve this hidden One when he chose to appear. Moreover he offered to baptize with water in the Jordan everyone who believed and was willing to enter the Kingdom which had already so quietly and wonderfully begun. Their baptism by water was a pledge that the Messiah himself would bring about their re-birth by the Holy Spirit. Many in the crowds responded to his call to receive baptism in the name of the coming one, and thus gave the sign that in heart and mind they were willing to forsake the ways of the present corrupt age, and desired the promised new life.

Simplicity and Wisdom

The Baptist was for a time successful and popular. The great crowds from all over the country who gathered to listen were impressed by his fearlessness, by the urgency of his message, and the passionate conviction with which he gave it. People began to think, to study the Scriptures, and to change their ways. Even some of the Pharisees, as Jesus later pointed out, "rejoiced for a while in his light" (John 5:35).

As his popularity grew, however, the leaders of the Jewish establishment in Jerusalem began to suspect that John might be one of these crazy people who from time to time disturbed the peace and led crowds astray by claiming falsely to be themselves the Messiah, the Christ. They sent messages to ask him if he made such a claim. John immediately denied the suggestion.

A series of other questions, however, followed. Moses, looking into the future had promised that God would one day raise up from among his people a prophet, a second Moses, whom his people were to heed (Deut. 18:15) – did John ever think of himself as fitting into such a prophecy? Or did he claim to be Elijah? Malachi, the last of the great prophets, at the end of his book had uttered the promise: "Behold I will send you Elijah before the great and terrible day of the Lord comes" (Mal. 4:5). Did John, in launching on his ministry and deciding his message, think of himself as called to fulfil this remakable promise?

John may have felt himself challenged by such questions. He must have asked himself if the texts they referred to really did describe the part and place given to him by God in the events leading up to the coming of the Messiah. The dress he adopted and the food he ate were reminiscent of Elijah (cf. Mark 1:6) and his location in the desert (like a second Moses) were signs that in beginning his ministry his thought had moved in this direction. Moreover, we know that Jesus, later on, looking over the events that led to his own baptism, taught that John was indeed the Elijah (Matt. 11:14) who was the forerunner of the true Messiah.

The unexpected answer which he now gave to his questioners, therefore casts some light for us on the kind of man he

was and on his attitude in his ministry. Even though he had
given some thought to such questions, he had refused to allow
his mind to dwell on them because to him they had become
superficial and purely speculative. He had concerned himself
completely with doing faithfully the one central task he knew
himself called to do in the service of God – proclaiming the
Kingdom and the coming One. He wanted nothing that might
divert him from this, or tempt him to become too concerned to
play up to an expected role. He wanted his hearers and questioners not to speculate over his identity and character as a
preacher, but to repent. He therefore gave an answer which he
hoped would draw attention away from his style and manner
of preaching to the urgency and content of his message. He
refused to be drawn into the discussion they were seeking. He
wanted his would-be examiners to forget the preacher and to
think about the Word.

We can recognize the trap that John was seeking to avoid,
and can appreciate the sheer wisdom and singleness of
purpose which shone out in his attitude before his questioners.
Too often in this respect we fail. Those of us who are called to
a ministry within the Church can become so concerned to
conform ourselves to the traditional role which we feel is
expected of us that we neglect what is more essential to our
task. Even in the conduct of the evangelistic service the
preacher can indulge in role-playing at the cost of true effectiveness. Hearers sometimes decide the worth of the message
by evaluating the personality, style or way of life of the one
who brings it.

Realism and Faith

In reply to further interrogation from his persistent
questioners, " *Who are you?* ", John quoted the well known text:
*"I am the voice of one crying in the wilderness, 'Make straight the way
of the Lord', as the prophet Isaiah said."*

When the prophet to whom he was referring originally
spoke these words he was calling on the people of God after
seventy years in exile in Babylon to prepare themselves for a
great miracle to happen in their wilderness surroundings.

Far away in a kingdom remote from them, Cyrus, the King

of Persia, was meanwhile setting out on a campaign that was to bring about the complete destruction of the Babylonian emperor and lead to their liberation.

Long before there was any evidence that such a deliverance was to happen, God gave the prophet the task of announcing it. He used poetical language. God, he said, was going to come and reveal his glory, preparing a way for them in the wilderness, levelling every mountain and exalting every valley so that they could soon go back to their own homeland over the deserts to start again in the service of God.

The people in Babylon when they heard his "good news" easily dismissed it from their minds. How could such a way be opened up? How could they ever expect the glory of God to be revealed in their dreadful and despondent situation? Facing their unbelief the prophet himself felt all the more how indefensible his message, how frail his voice, how weak his cry, dying out so soon in the vast wilderness spaces!

Yet within a few months they were to find that the voice that had seemed to create nothing more than an empty echo in the wasteland around them was going to prove itself the very Word of God, going forth with power into history to effect one of God's great redemptive purposes!

The Baptist, in his choice of this text to describe himself and his situation to his questioners showed that he was taking a sober and entirely realistic view of his ministry and its limitations. He knew that, like Isaiah, he himself could be suspected of merely throwing into the wilderness empty words that could effect nothing. He himself, too, in despondent moments may have been tempted to share this view of his preaching. After all, what evidence had he that anything more was at issue? The same realistic admission of the apparent limitation of everything he was doing comes out in his further reply to their question put to him about his baptism: "*I baptize with water*".

Mere *voice*! Mere *water*! He claims nothing more. Possibly he was too acutely conscious of his own personal unworthiness to do so. Certainly he did not boast (though a more foolish man might have done so) about the large numbers who were coming to the Jordan, their ardent enthusiasm, and the signs of genuine repentance that were evident.

He was only too aware that numbers can mean nothing, that human enthusiasm can soon fade, and that the signs of success can often be ambiguous. Yet the faith he expressed in these very utterances looked to the future with serene confidence. His own *voice crying in the wilderness* of Judaea would soon prove itself no less true and effective as a Word of God than that which, uttered among the Babylonian wastes, brought about the re-birth of the people of God centuries before. From day to day he looked forward with increasing ardour to the appearance of One whom he knew would come to claim him, to take over his work, to baptize with the Holy Spirit, and to pronounce the only verdict worth listening to.

How little we ourselves sometimes have to show or speak about, when we face the world and its questioning: '*a voice . . . water*' – bread and wine! Even when there is a crowd around us to watch and listen, it is so obviously a mere crowd of ordinary people! But how much we have in the now hidden present and glorious future to be confident about, to rejoice and even to boast in!

No Answer

We can trace an element of uneasiness in the pressure which John's questioners exert for definite information about himself, "*Let us have an answer for those who sent us*". John has been deliberately enigmatic and his final answers simply deepen the mystery.

Here we are at the beginning of a conflict which runs through the whole of John's Gospel, and continually comes to the surface – the conflict caused by the reaction of the darkness prevailing in the world to the light which has come to take over in Jesus. The stage is set for the appearance of Jesus, and the chosen first witness is there ready to welcome and proclaim him. But before he even appears in public the opposition is also there alert and determined even in its perplexity. The questioning of the Baptist is to be regarded as a form of inquisition, for suspicion and fear have been aroused.

Perhaps it is because he senses their hostility that John is so careful and indirect in his answers. It is fitting that in their anxiety the authorities should be shown up as unable to grasp what they are opposing, for they are doomed to be over-whelmed by something they are incapable of comprehending (cf. 1:5) Here there is at work the wisdom of God which "none of the rulers of this world understood", says Paul, "for if they had, they would not have crucified the Lord of Glory". (1 Cor. 2:8).

CHAPTER 3

THE BAPTIST AND JESUS
John 1:29 – 38

29 The next day he saw Jesus coming towards him, and said, "Behold, the Lamb of God, who takes away the sin of the world! [30]This is he of whom I said, 'After me comes a man who ranks before me, for he was before me.' [31]I myself did not know him; but for this I came baptizing with water, that he might be revealed to Israel." [32]And John bore witness, "I saw the Spirit descend as a dove from heaven, and it remained on him. [33]I myself did not know him: but he who sent me to baptize with water said to me, 'He on whom you see the Spirit descend and remain, this is he who baptizes with the Holy Spirit.' [34]And I have seen and have borne witness that this is the Son of God."

35 The next day again John was standing with two of his disciples: [36]and he looked at Jesus as he walked, and said, "Behold, the Lamb of God!" [37]The two disciples heard him say this, and they followed Jesus. [38]Jesus turned, and saw them following.

The Reorientation of a Ministry

The crowd which gathered on one particular day to hear the Baptist must have been astonished at the sudden change in his message and tone. In place of the usual vivid descriptions of the catastrophic changes threatening history, there was the story of what he had heard and seen as he had baptized Jesus. Instead of the call "Repent and flee from the wrath to come" they heard the call to give the devotion of their minds and

15

hearts to the one who had come to be their Messiah, there now walking in humility among them.

From the moment Jesus had approached him for baptism John had sensed that he was on the verge of the revelation they had all for so long been waiting for. The hidden Messiah had now declared himself. John had felt awe in the presence of one "the thong of whose sandal I am not worthy to untie". The vision that he had then had by the Jordan played a large part in determining his whole future prophetic ministry. Jesus had demanded baptism. John had obeyed him. The heavens had been opened, he had seen the Spirit descending like a dove on Jesus, and he had heard the voice of God declaring the very presence on earth, to begin his reign, of his beloved Son. At that moment he had come to know with complete certainty why he had been raised up by God to be his prophet. He had to bear witness to what he had seen and heard in his encounter with Jesus. He had to plead with all around to look, to enter the fellowship offered in his presence, so that they too might hear and see for themselves that *this is the Son of God*.

Moreover, the sight of Jesus, the Son of God, submitting himself in such deep humility to a sinner's baptism transformed everything he now had to say about what God's Messiah had come into the world to do and achieve. In his preaching up to this moment he had drawn pictures of him as he had thought he found him in Scripture – of a Lord glorious in visible majesty, no one able to stand alongside him, compelling submission and obedience whenever he willed. But Jesus had now shown himself a Messiah humble, gentle, dedicated to self sacrifice. By submitting himself to baptism alongside repentant sinners in all their need he had recalled to John's mind how the coming one was described in other parts of Scripture – especially in the fifty-third chapter of Isaiah. He was to be the Servant of God who had come to number himself with the transgressors in self-condemnation and confession of sin. He had come to pour out his soul to death in intercession for those whose sins he had come thus to bear. He was going to allow himself to be "led to the slaughter" as the Passover Lamb was slain so that it might set God's people free. *"Behold the Lamb of God"*, cried John, pointing to Jesus, *"who takes away the sin of the world!"* (cf. Isa. 53, Exod 12:1 – 3).

Of course, as John continued to preach and baptize during the weeks or months that lay ahead, the other themes that had up till now been central to his ministry continued to reappear in what he said – the warnings of the approaching end of the world, the call to renounce the ways and aims of the present age, the demands for uprightness in heart and in personal dealings each with his neighbour, the call to repent and be baptized. Indeed he preached on such things with all the more force and certainty than ever before because Jesus himself had given such aspects of his former ministry wholehearted approval by coming to receive his Baptism of repentance and to confirm the truth of his witness.

Yet there can be no doubt that on whatever aspect of life he preached, the Word of God was now for him the Word made flesh in Jesus of Nazareth the Son of God, who had come amongst us in his grace to take away the sin of the world. This now gave him a new central point for all his thought about his message and his mission. It also gave him a new motive in all his appeals for political reform, social justice, and personal repentance. It was for the sake of this man that the world must now be purged of the evils that hindered the coming of his Kingdom, and robbed him of his rightful rule over everything in the universe. It was only as they devoted themselves to the service and fellowship of this man, came under his influence, understood their indebtedness to him, that John now believed the world could be purged of its evils. Only as he was given his rightful personal place in the hearts and minds of men and women could the Kingdom of God come, could people begin to understand themselves, the true meaning of life, and the true nature of God.

Take-over and Surrender

Amongst the crowds who came to hear John, there were those especially close to him who had come most deeply under his influence – his *"disciples"*. Jesus is pictured here as deliberately drawing into his own service two of these men. John himself is shown as not only freely surrendering them, but also as initiating the movement that was to deprive himself of them.

Pastoral conversation between the preacher and his hearers
is often a valuable part of church life. It is sometimes required
to clarify impressions that are too hazy, and to clinch the
message. Such a conversation was taking place. John was re-
telling what he had seen and heard. No doubt the two were
asking questions. As they were speaking together, Jesus came
again in view. He seemed, indeed, to bring himself within an
engaging distance of them, and John could point to him as he
had done in his sermon on the day before. *"Behold the Lamb of
God"* John said. This time he makes no direct reference to the
way Jesus has chosen to meet the sin of the world. He is
dwelling at this particular point in the conversation not
primarily on the sacrifice that is finally to prove and seal God's
love, but on what has impressed him about the man Jesus
himself – the one whom God has sent.

We cannot of course separate Jesus from his Cross. But the
"Lamb" himself, and purely for his own sake, is as worthy of
open-hearted contemplation and adoration as the Cross for
which he is destined. "Behold the Lamb without blemish!"
(cf. Exod. 12:5), the Baptist is saying. He had known him
from childhood, and had admired him as a person – a man
pure, true, humble, untainted in character and aim by the
vicious devouring world, a leader worthy of complete
devotion and trust! There is a truth enshrined in hymns like
"Fairest Lord Jesus" that makes them of great value in our
worship.

The two disciples, as they looked, felt drawn to the man
there within their view. They yielded, and the transfer from
one leader to another took place quietly and without fuss. No
formal farewell or acknowledgement of debt to John is
recorded: *They heard John speak and they followed Jesus.* What
happened at this moment was John's greatest achievement,
the climax of his ministry. The two friends to whom he spoke
found at last everything they had hoped that life would give
them. Jesus found his first disciples. The Christian Church
began to take shape. No doubt there were other memorable
days when the crowds around were very great, the word
seemed especially inspired, and the response astonished ob-
servers. But did anything greater happen because of his
witness than here, so quietly, unnoticed by anyone else, when

the two disciples heard John speak and they followed the one of whom he spoke? The Kingdom of God, said Jesus, comes not with observation (Luke 17:20). A later commentator looking back on the whole ministry of the Baptist made the comment: "John did no sign, but everything John said about this man was true" (John 10:41).

It was an act of deliberate and costly self-denial on John's part to open up to Jesus, in this way, the whole sphere in which he had been the leading and guiding light and influence. John well knew that even the part he had played in introducing his disciples to Jesus would soon be forgotten, and they would begin to talk as if they by themselves had found what he had introduced to them (cf. v.41). It is not easy to find those we have toiled to care for and educate, on whom perhaps we have learned to some extent to depend, beginning to grow careless towards us because they have found something that can give them more satisfaction in life, and a better direction, than we ourselves could ever have offered had they stayed with us. John was content, as long as what happened bore witness to the light that had come into the world in Jesus.

Jesus Christ is the Same Yesterday and Today and For Ever

Though we are meant to admire the self-effacement and faithful witnessing of John, we are meant to note especially in the latter part of this incident the decisive part played by Jesus himself. He is about to begin his own ministry. He needs disciples. He wants to start with these two men. He is aware that he is being talked about, and is sensitive to their thoughts and inclinations as they listen to John. He watches for the response and anticipates their approach to him, by himself turning from his way so that he and they can meet face to face.

At this point we can begin to notice also how directly relevant the Gospel story is to our present-day life, and how easy it is to move in thought from Jesus and his disciples in that world of past history, to the presence of the living and risen Jesus in the Church world of today. We need not doubt that all these things we have been reading about happened as history when Jesus Christ was there in the flesh. Yet what we have read seems at times intentionally designed to tell us not only about what once happened there and then, but also about what is happening, and can happen, between Jesus and ourselves today.

One recent scholar has strongly affirmed his belief that in some incidents, the narrative in John's Gospel was deliberately constructed to describe the action of the Risen Christ during Eucharistic worship in the early church. However this may be, it is certainly true that many of the Gospel stories here and elsewhere are about "Jesus Christ . . . the same yesterday and today and forever" (Heb. 13:8). Indeed Jesus later remarked that what he did to the disciples when he washed their feet in the upper room would only be fully understood by them when he came back to have dealings with them after his resurrection (John 13:7). Are there not other incidents in the Gospel story to the meaning of which we can find our best clue in what Jesus himself is doing in our midst today? We can therefore allow this incident to bring before our mind the later promise of Jesus : "where two or three are gathered in my name there am I in the midst of them" (Matt. 18:20).

Where the preacher or teacher today seeks to give the same faithful witness as did the Baptist in his day, speaks of the man, the sacrifice, the presence, of what he demands and offers today, Jesus himself will come near as he came to these three at the Jordan. He has the same delicate sensitivity as he had then to every thought of a mind that is turning towards his light, and he will put himself within the reach of the least desire that is kindled in a longing heart by the promises of his presence and power. Is there not in this text the assurance that there can and will take place today in our midst, the eternally significant take-over: *They heard him preach and they followed Jesus?*

We need not confine our application of this incident to what takes place between Pastor and congregation. Indeed, the fact that the group consisted only of three is an encouragement to apply it to the Sunday School teacher, or to the study leader in a Church group, or to the pastoral counsellor, or to the mother in the home who may have only two, or perhaps one little one, beside her, but who knows that it is vain for our children to have everything that life can give, if they do not have Christ.

We can at least hope and pray that, whatever the circumstances, this quiet and binding encounter and commitment may go on continually within the life of the Church.

CHAPTER 4

JESUS AND HIS FIRST DISCIPLES
John 1:37 – 51

It is worth while, as we go through this passage, to note the different ways in which Jesus dealt with different disciples of John on his first introduction to them. In each case we can assume that there took place a quite decisive meeting, bringing sudden and deep commitment to Jesus and his service. Yet the level and type of immediate experience, the degree of spiritual insight, and the confession of faith arising out of the experience, vary. Each individual has a unique temperament and character, and Jesus himself has his own special way with each one he meets.

Jesus, Andrew and John

John 1:37 – 39

[37]The two disciples heard him say this, and they followed Jesus. [38]Jesus turned, and saw them following and said to them, "What do you seek?" And they said to him, "Rabbi" (which means Teacher), "where are you staying?" [39]He said to them, "Come and see." They came and saw where he was staying: and they stayed with him that day, for it was about the tenth hour.

As the two disciples made up on Jesus, he faced them with a question meant to be all the more searching and disturbing because it was put so abruptly and seriously. *"What do you seek?"*

It was a question about the strength and purity of their motives for seeking to enter his service. Obviously they had become attracted to his person. They were also deeply

22

interested in his cause and the way he is going to take to fulfil it. But what did they really expect to find in it? How far indeed will they let themselves be led on when the cost involves persecution and the difficulties seem overwhelming? He does not want to steal loyalty by false pretence, nor to trap people into his service by delusive, superficial charm.

Jesus had not yet spoken of the cost of becoming a disciple, or of the purity of heart, the singleness of purpose and the utter carelessness of self-interest which he expected his followers to seek under his influence. Nor had he yet described the great and thrilling rewards they would receive. Yet in his presence even at this early stage in his ministry they must have felt to some extent the issues and constraints that later became explicit in his teaching. They were disturbed by the questions of conscience and the sense of unworthiness which is felt in all genuine human encounter with Jesus. His presence itself was searching. They felt that deceit or reserve were impossible.

The answer which Jesus' abrupt question evoked is striking: "*Rabbi, where are you staying?*" It is an answer that he himself inspires. In his presence they find themselves accepted, and drawn on. They do not shrink from the light in which they have had to begin uncomfortably to question themselves. They want more of it. They want to go on with him and to know him better. They make no attempt at self-assessment or even confession, for they want *him* to tell them who and what they are.

Moreover, the Baptist, by his description of what happened to him with Jesus at Jordan when "the heavens were opened" had aroused in them a desire also to see. Might they too in their encounter here with Jesus not be on the threshold of the kind of vision and experience which had so transformed the life and ministry of their friend John? They want to probe further.

In the way they worded their reply, a healthy desire is expressed for what is down-to-earth and permanent. Their first aim is not some once-for-all mystical encounter with heavenly reality which leaves them momentarily excited and impressed, and perhaps suddenly changed. They know themselves, rather, to be entering a lasting friendship with a person at whose address they can find him again and again.

They call him *"Rabbi" (which means Teacher)* for they believe he
has a store of wisdom from which they will gradually learn.
They will surrender to him the mind, as well as the will of the
heart.

Jesus, having inspired their manifold prayer immediately
*said to them "Come and see." They came and saw where he was
staying; and they stayed with him that day.*

We must of course, interpret this in the first place on a quite
mundane level. He took them to his lodgings and they spent
the rest of the day with him. They now had his home address,
the promise of easy access when they want to find him. There
was too, in this gesture, the promise of personal friendship. If
they have questions and problems, his mind and heart will be
as open to them as his lodgings were.

Reading this incident in the context of the whole of John's
Gospel, however, it is natural that our thoughts should move
to a level of meaning which the writer often had in mind.
When Jesus said *"Come and see,"* was he not seeking to answer
the desire which John the Baptist's testimony to the "Son"
and "Lamb" of God had raised in their minds and hearts?
Was he not hoping and praying that having stepped over the
threshold of his earthly lodgings they might come also to step
over another threshold to share something of the vision and
insight of their former leader?

When I was a divinity student in Edinburgh it was a
coincidence that on two occasions on our "retreats" members
of the faculty chose this passage from John's Gospel as the
basis of their talk to us about our ministry. Both of them
pointed out that it was unusual for John to mention the exact
time of day in relation to any incident, yet here we had it: *it was
about four in the afternoon* (NEB). Their explanation was that for
John what happened as he came to know Jesus on that visit
was so memorable and of such lasting significance he could
not forbear to mention significantly in the Gospel that exact
time of the day. It was the hour when *they came and saw where he
was staying.* Might there not have been, there and then,
indeed a moment of new and unforgettable insight into who
Jesus really was and where he really belonged? From this hour
on they began to see that this man Jesus dwelt not only in these
lodgings, but was also, as he later describes himself, 'the Son of

Man whose home is in Heaven' (John 3:13 NEB). In Scotland they used to speak of certain godly men or women as being "far ben with God". In a quite unique and realistic way this was where Jesus was, and this was what they "saw".

There are further suggestive overtones in this remarkable text as we have it. Throughout the text, and in the comment, *"they stayed with him that day"* one Greek verb is used which as well as being translated "stay" can be translated "dwell" or "abide". The same word is later used in the Gospel to refer to our indwelling or abiding in Christ. As one recent commentator says: "The abiding of the disciples with Jesus anticipates their abiding in Him even as He abides in the Father." This aspect of the text further underlines the permanence and stability of the relationship which Jesus comes to set up between ourselves and him, and thus between ourselves and God.

It was one of the vexations felt by men in the Old Testament times that their visitations by God and their experiences of confident faith were at times so transitory – even though they had their temple services through which to find him, and the Law and the Prophets through which to hear his voice. Jeremiah once put the complaint this way:

"O Thou hope of Israel
its Saviour in time of trouble,
Why should'st thou be like a stranger in the land,
like a wayfarer who turns aside to tarry for a
night?" (14:8).

It is true that even in the fellowship which we have with the risen Jesus under the New Covenant, there still remains an element of the same transitoriness (cf. Luke 24:31). We can never localize God or try to hold his presence down anywhere or anyhow. But when Jesus said "Seek and you will find, knock and it will be opened to you" (Matt. 7:7), he is reminding us that now there is an address, a door, through knocking at which, we have a more sure promise of finding him present to us today, than ever anyone had before. He sets before us today the Gospel story, and the witness of all the Apostles to what they have seen and heard, and the Sacraments, his special extra gifts to the believing Church.

Here is his address. Here is the door. Here he invites us to
seek, to knock, to wait and to enter so that we can continually
abide in him, as he seeks to abide in us.

Jesus and Peter

John 1:40 – 42

[40]One of the two who heard John speak, and followed
him, was Andrew, Simon Peter's brother. [41]He first
found his brother Simon and said to him, "We have
found the Messiah" (which means Christ). [42]He
brought him to Jesus. Jesus looked at him, and said, "So
you are Simon the son of John? You shall be called
Cephas" (which means Peter).

Of course Andrew, as soon as he could, told the news of this
meeting with Jesus to *his brother Simon*, and lost no time in
bringing him to Jesus. He must have been disappointed that
with Peter, Jesus did not take the same approach, or make the
same immediate effort as he had with himself and John. Little
time was taken there and then, no questions were asked, and
Jesus was content to dismiss him, with simply one word, *"So
you are Simon the son of John? You shall be called Cephas (which means
Peter)."* Peter himself possibly had come with greater
expectations.

Yet the word spoken by Jesus was a Word of God – "It
shall not return to me empty, but it shall accomplish that
which I purpose and prosper in the thing for which I sent it!"
(Isa. 55:11). We can read of its magnificent fulfilment in the
great moment of vision, discovery and public confession of
Jesus as the Christ, the Son of the Living God at Caesarea
Philippi, when Jesus himself was thrilled at the faith and gift of
leadership which his Father had given to this elect disciple
(Matt 16:13 – 20). We can read, too, of the long struggle
between the old Simon and the new Peter in this one man as he
followed Jesus. It was a struggle which went on even till the
time of his final denial of Jesus (John 18:25), and his final re-
affirmation of his loyalty and his restoration by Jesus at the
lakeside (John 21:15 – 19).

Nothing of what was to happen was known when the Word that brought it about was first spoken. It is an encouragement to all of us who cannot tell, as others seem to be able to do, any dramatic story of what we saw and experienced as the beginning of our Christian life. All that may have come to us at that period was simply the impression, from what we had heard or read of Jesus and his Words, that in him we were faced with the Truth – an impression confirmed by the testimonies we heard from friends and relatives whom we respect and trust. Even now we may have nothing much more to grasp than the many promises and assuring words which have come home to us through the Word of God which holds us to our faith in him and in what he has done for us. Within us there may be simply a steady and growing conviction that in following and trusting we have a future, a destiny, and that the world, too, has its destiny only in him. "We walk by faith, not by sight" wrote Paul (2 Cor. 5:7). It is on Christ's decision, Christ's word, and not on the experience he grants us that the future depends. Experience is his gift and he does not fail to bring comfort when his people need it. In the working out of our Christian way, long-run perseverance is of more importance than great moments of initial excitement.

Jesus and Philip

John 1:43 – 46

[43]The next day Jesus decided to go to Galilee. And he found Philip and said to him, "Follow me." [44]Now Philip was from Bethsaida, the city of Andrew and Peter. [45]Philip found Nathanael, and said to him, "We have found him of whom Moses in the law and also the prophets wrote, Jesus of Nazareth, the son of Joseph." [46]Nathanael said to him, "Can anything good come out of Nazareth?" Philip said to him, "Come and see."

Philip began enthusiastically and did well. He was keen to share what he had seen and found, even in that first short personal encounter when Jesus came seeking him. "*Come and see*", he said to Nathanael. Later on it was he who contacted the Greeks who wanted to see Jesus (John 12:21 – 22). Jesus seemed to be on familiar terms and free in his conversation with him (John 6:4 – 7). Of course he was there with the others in the upper room at the Last Supper, and along with Thomas was disarmingly frank in expressing the difficulties he had in understanding what Jesus was talking about.

It was at that crucial moment, however, that Jesus expressed disappointment that Philip still remained unaware of much that Jesus had hoped he would have learned and seen: "Have I been with you so long and yet do you not know me, Philip?" (John 14:9)

It is certainly hazardous to try to guess what it was that, during this first encounter, fascinated Philip, and made him say, "*Come and see!*" yet it is possible that he found so much attractive and great simply in Jesus as a man, that he settled down with it, and made no great effort even to ask if there was more to discover. He had been looking for no more than could be found on a human level, and he was too soon satisfied. The unreality which he confessed to have found in Jesus' talk about the Father, even in the upper room confirms this suspicion.

However satisfying our new found faith, however deep our new insights may seem to be, the beginning is always meant to be simply a beginning. However much we might have already seen, there is more to see, and what we have seen has to be allowed to unfold itself through time, so that we can understand it more clearly, and it comes to have all the greater effect on our temperament and our way of life.

Jesus and Nathanael

John 1:45 – 51

[45]Philip found Nathanael, and said to him, "We have found him of whom Moses in the law and also the prophets wrote, Jesus of Nazareth, the son of Joseph". [46]Nathanael said to him, "Can anything good come out of Nazareth?" Philip said to him, "Come and see." [47]Jesus saw Nathanael coming to him, and said of him, "Behold, an Israelite indeed, in whom is no guile!"

⁴⁸Nathanael said to him "How do you know me?" Jesus answered him, "Before Philip called you, when you were under the fig tree, I saw you." ⁴⁹Nathanael answered him, "Rabbi, you are the Son of God! You are the King of Israel!" ⁵⁰Jesus answered him, "Because I said to you, I saw you under the fig tree, do you believe? You shall see greater things than these." ⁵¹And he said to him, "Truly, truly, I say to you, you will see heaven opened, and the angels of God ascending and descending upon the Son of man."

Jesus' first words to Nathanael must have seemed to an onlooker like Philip completely enigmatic: "*Behold an Israelite indeed, in whom is no guile!*"

From Nathanael himself, however, it brought a cry of astonished wonder. Here was someone who, before he had even talked to him, seemed already to have read his heart, heard his secret and ardent prayer, and had an answer to it! One of the Psalmists in the Old Testament one day suddenly found himself overwhelmed by the realisation of the intimate knowledge the all-seeing and all-knowing God had of him, of how close and personal he was, how inescapable and holy: "O Lord thou hast searched me and known me! Thou knowest when I sit down and when I rise up; Thou discernest my thoughts from afar" (139:1, 2). As Nathanael, perhaps gradually, took in the full meaning of Jesus' word to him, he expressed his feelings in a phrase that echoed something of the Psalmist's wonder before the all-seeing God. How was it that this man had come to such a perfect understanding of the whole tenor of his inner desire and thought?

The exact way in which Jesus' strange remark proved that he had this intimate knowledge of the thoughts of Nathanael's mind and the desires of his heart, is not explained here in detail, but clear hints are given throughout the whole conversation of the points at which Nathanael felt himself deeply and sensitively touched.

We must assume that Nathanael was a sincere and ardent student of the Word of God who read it in depth and allowed the full searching challenge of its teaching to penetrate his heart and to dominate his personal life in all its aspects. Jesus' remark, "*Behold an Israelite indeed, in whom is no guile*", was made with the clear implication that Nathanael had been thinking about Jacob, the story of whom is *the* story of deliverance from the guilt and power of guile. It was also made with the implication that one of the blessings Nathanael ardently sought was that promised in the 32nd Psalm: "Blessed is the man to whom the Lord imputes no iniquity, and in whose spirit there is no deceit" (Ps. 32:2). This had been Nathanael's deepest problem as he had tried sincerely to serve God and to prepare himself to meet the Messiah, and it had surfaced strongly and perhaps tormentingly in his mind at the moment of his encounter with Jesus. Here was Jesus revealing that he understood, as only God can understand, the innermost drift of the secret thoughts of the man before him.

The word spoken by Jesus was intended not simply to uncover Nathanael's personal problem, but to meet it. It was meant to be heard by Nathanael as a word of assurance and grace. His problem had been a burden on his conscience. Jesus had come to lift it. We can remember how later on, the word of Jesus to the leper, "Be clean" brought immediate cleansing and wholeness. In the same powerful way, the word of Jesus, "*Behold an Israelite without guile!*" came to Nathanael as a declaration of forgiveness and liberty which brought immediate inner release, and an answer to years of prayer.

The awe which Nathanael felt in the presence of Jesus was deepened by a second remark in reply to his first expression of astonishment. There was a current tradition that the ideal Israelite in the Messianic age would go at times to meditate, "each under his fig tree" (cf. Mic. 4:4, Zech 3:10). There may have been a fig tree somewhere in his garden where Nathanael had just been seeking to prepare himself in prayer for the coming new age, or it may have been that just before the time of Jesus' approach with Philip, Nathanael had in imagination thought of himself in that setting. Jesus said to him: "*Before Philip called you, when you were under the fig tree, I saw you.*"

Nathanael tried to express his continuing wonder at what has happened in a confession of faith: "*Rabbi you are the Son of God! You are the King of Israel!*" Commentators warn us not to read too much theology into his confession. Nathanael, they warn us, is here addressing Jesus as "*Teacher*", and in the titles "*Son of God*" and "*King of Israel*" he is simply acknowledging that he is the Messiah. Yet, even though the confession may be read in this superficial way there can be no doubt that Nathanael believes that in Jesus the eternal God himself has come close to him with redeeming power, and he is seeking to give an adequate confession of this faith.

We are meant to notice, in passing, the initial mental barrier which Nathanael raised when Philip first spoke of Jesus. "*Can any good thing come out of Nazareth?*" It was a piece of local prejudice that made life occasionally difficult for those who came from the place. Of course it would indicate to us a rather sad initial defect in the character of Nathanael. Such cultural snobbery seems incompatible with genuine personal piety. Indeed, it is such cultural prejudice, void of any rational basis, that is the origin of racism with its devastating modern effects. We ourselves are therefore apt to judge those who harbour even a suspicion of it more harshly than they themselves judge the victims of their own minds. Yet in Nathanael's case Jesus showed no reverse prejudice against the prejudice! In some cases the heart can be genuine even though the outlook is warped! He looked at the heart and was able to overlook for a moment even this defect. Where he finds faith and an earnest desire for communion with himself he is prepared to enter that close relationship with people which can ultimately melt away everything that cuts us off from each other.

A Final Word

John 1:50 – 51

[50]Jesus answered him, "Because I said to you, I saw you under the fig tree, do you believe? You shall see greater things than these." [51]And he said to him, "Truly, truly, I say to you, you will see heaven opened, and the angels of God ascending and descending upon the Son of man."

Jesus' final word in this chapter was, of course, especially to Nathanael. He is referring him again to the story of Jacob, the man who ultimately, delivered from guile, became the true Israel. Jacob even early in his career was granted the great vision of a ladder stretched from heaven to earth and the angels of God ascending and descending on it. Nathanael is being challenged not to be content till through his fellowship with Jesus, such a vision is granted to him also. It is the same challenge which, the day before, Jesus had already given to Andrew and John with his invitation: "Come and see!"

John Calvin is correct in isolating this last verse from its immediate context and suggesting that it should be interpreted as a promise addressed by Jesus to all Christians who have begun each in his or her own way to follow Jesus. They should expect to happen to them what happened to Jacob at Bethel, what happened also to John the Baptist by the Jordan. Calvin is not suggesting that we should seek for the fulfilment of this promise in some kind of dream or visionary experience in which the pictorial detail of those former experiences is reproduced before our minds. The promise is, rather, a plea to us not to remain content with limited and low-level views of the significance of Jesus himself, but to seek the same kind of insight as made these early disciples worship him, and strain their language to find an adequate confession of who he is, and where he really belongs. In this word he is giving all of us the same challenge and the same promise as he had already given to Andrew and John: "Come and see."

CHAPTER 5

THE WEDDING AT CANA

John 2:1 – 11

2 On the third day there was a marriage at Cana in Galilee, and the mother of Jesus was there; [2]Jesus also was invited to the marriage, with his disciples. [3]When the wine failed, the mother of Jesus said to him, "They have no wine." [4]And Jesus said to her, "O woman, what have you to do with me? My hour has not yet come." [5]His mother said to the servants, "Do whatever he tells you." [6]Now six stone jars were standing there, for the Jewish rites of purification, each holding twenty or thirty gallons. [7]Jesus said to them, "Fill the jars with water." And they filled them up to the brim. [8]He said to them, "Now draw some out, and take it to the steward of the feast." So they took it. [9]When the steward of the feast tasted the water now become wine, and did not know where it came from (though the servants who had drawn the water knew), the steward of the feast called the bridegroom [10]and said to him, "Every man serves the good wine first; and when men have drunk freely, then the poor wine; but you have kept the good wine until now." [11]This, the first of his signs, Jesus did at Cana in Galilee, and manifested his glory; and his disciples believed in him.

Invitation to Local Celebration

We are meant to notice the contrast which suddenly appears here. In the first chapter of this Gospel we were introduced to Jesus as the one inspiring reverence, majestic in his bearing and his talk – the Only Son and Word of God. Here in this chapter we are reminded that he was indeed also the son of Mary, the man of Nazareth, our brother man in our humanity. We are shown how he loved his involvement in the social and family life of the towns and villages around Galilee. *There was a marriage at Cana in Galilee, and the mother of Jesus was there; Jesus also was invited to the marriage, with his disciples.*

That he accepted this invitation, given because he was a member of a family circle, reminds us of one of the features of the Gospel that should continually fill us with wonder and gratitude: that God has entered our human life in an intimate way. He has become like one of our family relations. He can be easily known and approached by us if we want him. He can be given an invitation to come and celebrate with us on happy family occasions. One of Augustine's prayers runs thus: "O God Thou hast set Thyself at but an handbreath from us, that we might seek Thee with a whole heart, and seeking Thee, find Thee."

There is a further contrast, of which we are meant to become more and more aware as we read through this incident. In the first chapter of the Gospel, Jesus is pointed to as "the Lamb of God who takes away the sin of the world". He knows himself called to a ministry characterized by self-denial, suffering and prayer. He has identified himself closely with John the Baptist, with his proclamation of the end of the world and the coming of the Kingdom of God, and his call to renounce the present age with its pride, ambitions, and sought-after pleasures. In this chapter, however, what he does at the wedding underlines his care for the immediate happiness of people around him who have little concern for his religious programme, and who are out simply for the pleasure it gives them to be at one of the happiest social occasions of the day. We see them here taking part not in the religious ceremony, but in the feasting – the secular part of the occasion which ordinary people in the world can appreciate and enjoy whether they are religious or not. He seems glad to be there, though for the most of the time he is entirely in the background and appears not to be needed. Yet when he is called on, he is there to give marvellous help.

It is good that we should pause for a moment to take in the

full significance of the central point we want to make in our approach to this passage. The Bible, in its stories about our beginnings tells us that after Adam and Eve fell, and were cast out of the garden, they were treated with tender consideration. God was gracious even to the family of Cain, the most disobedient son of Adam. It was to members of this family that were given special skills in music and the arts and sciences. God indeed wanted to make life not only bearable but happy and rich for them while he waited as he had to, to send his Son into the world to save them. Therefore even while they lived at enmity against God he nevertheless gave them all the gifts they required to enable them, if they wanted to, to develop a good human secular culture and civilisation.

These old stories are there to show us in simple and vivid pictures how we are to think about our human situation today. God today through innumerable signs, shows his goodness not only to those who believe in him, but also to the whole human race. We know that whether we are Christians or not we can enjoy and find use for many good secular gifts in such things as music, the arts and sciences. We are meant to be thankful for such gifts to humanity, even though we often abuse them. Jesus meant us to recognize this when he reminded us that the heavenly Father makes his sun rise on the evil and the good, and sends rain on the just and upon the unjust (Matt. 5:45).

Of all the good gifts God wants all humankind to enjoy while they live on earth – whether they believe in him or not – one of the greatest and most to be prized is the gift of marriage. Where on earth, within the vast range of interesting and joyful occasions which occur for celebration in our ordinary secular lives can there be any human joy so great and good as that in which we share by being present at a wedding reception? Can we have any clearer proof that anyone has become stupid or inhuman than to find him refusing the invitation to a wedding because he wants to go to a football match or to a symphony concert? The height of social privilege is to be invited to a wedding. The height of social joy is to be there as a welcome guest – and there was Jesus Christ, in quite secular company.

An Ever-recurring Human Situation

It starts off well – the dancing, the clapping, the feasting, the laughing. Jeremiah, thinking back to the good days of his youth, remembered at weddings, "the voice of mirth and the voice of gladness, the voice of the bridegroom and the voice of the bride". (Jer. 16:9, 25:10) It is all the more spontaneous within this community where they know each other so well. The pace of the affair is mounting and everything that is happening promises so much!

Yet a flaw appeared and a threat occurred – the wine began to fail! It was very strange that this should happen at an affair so carefully planned. Had some of the jars been cracked or faulty? Could those responsible for the catering have badly miscalculated? (Some commentators suggest that the guests themselves were expected to provide the wine by bringing gifts with them, and that perhaps people like Jesus had let them down!)

Whatever our mind suggests as the immediate cause of the shortage we are meant to recognize the seriousness of the situation which arose as a result. The wine at this wedding had great importance in the minds of those concerned, and its failure was bound to have deep significance. These were superstitious days and this was a very ordinary crowd of people. The failure of the wine if it had taken place would not only have been a ridiculous anti-climax, a sad and stupid sudden ending to the great day, and a kind of family disgrace; it would have been interpreted as a portent, a shadow hanging over the couple all their days. The situation was one of real crisis – indeed of threatened tragedy.

Moreover the situation was made all the more tragic and absurd by the fact that the wine began to fail quite suddenly and unexpectedly at the high point of the success of the party. They were having the time of their lives when suddenly with dismay and alarm, in deep anxiety and desperate frustration those who are responsible go to Mary the mother of Jesus and speak of the shadow that is about to fall on this great gathering, "Can you believe it Mary? The wine is running out!" They are apprehensive for the whole future of the marriage itself.

Is the situation which occurred at this wedding not very

familiar today to those of us who are able to enjoy life as we are meant to do in an affluent society? In what we have around us in our ordinary day to day lives within our families, our culture and society, we can find much that brings us joy. There is beauty and goodness in many aspects of our human intercourse. We can admire what talented people with their God-given gifts can produce for our pleasure. They add colour to life. We sometimes say "Life is sweet". Moreover, in spite of all the threats and dangers which science brings, we have to be thankful for the progress it has brought in easing our drudgery, in spreading entertainment, in overcoming ill-health.

And yet, within such a situation do we not at times come to the point of utter and pathetic crisis? The wine threatens to run out, and what has seemed so real and exciting appears to be empty, insipid, and meaningless. Life with its sweetness and goodness suddenly reveals its vanity. The ground which we had felt secure suddenly gives way beneath us, and even we, too, of the 20th century, have our forebodings about what is to happen.

The crisis can indeed come suddenly upon us – like the coming of the thieves in Jesus' parable who without warning "break in and steal" (Matt. 6:19). Illness can strike, disaster can happen, bereavement can come quickly and shatteringly. More often, however, we become aware of ourselves moving towards it gradually. The moth and rust consume! (Matt. 6:19) Strength ebbs, beauty fades, and the mind grows feeble. The fact that the crisis at Cana took place at a wedding reception reminds us of how often it happens today, suddenly or slowly, in our marriages. However great the early happiness, however binding the vows, so often, after few or many years, in a home bereft of everything they have hoped for, the man and the woman find they have to face each other and the situation: "We have no wine!"

Perhaps there is something in the structure of life itself which makes us sense the approach of the crisis before it comes upon us. We remember the story of the little girl at the pantomime, so thrilled at what she was enjoying, and then suddenly clutching her mother's arm: "It's not going to end soon, is it Mummy?" Solomon after all his efforts to ensure he was surrounded by everything that could ensure his well-being and pleasure, makes his confession: "Then I considered all that my hands had done and the toil I had spent in doing it, and behold all was vanity and a striving after wind." (Eccl. 2:11) As someone once put it, "The word 'enjoy' comes to have no strength in it."

The world of politics is not exempt. Too often the hopes invested in radical change towards the right or the left are soon dashed, and it becomes a relief to disillusioned followers and voters that there is some other administration ready in the wings to take over. A recent review of books on the French Revolution remarked: "There can be no doubt that the noble ideals which characterized its early stages were soon perverted."

The Hidden Sign

Jesus, appealed to by his mother, answered her prayer and enabled the celebration to go on. It was a miracle done without fuss or ceremony, almost in secrecy. It is emphasised throughout the story that Jesus did not have any prominence at any time among the guests and even to the end remained only in the background. The praise for the wine therefore went to others. How unusual to serve such perfect wine towards the end of the feast, when people who had already drunk so much were all the less able to appreciate it! The Steward of the feast complimented the Bridegroom and the implication is that even the Bridegroom, accepting the compliment no doubt gratefully, was unaware of what was happening around him. At this moment, even when they were praising each other for the goodness and joy of it, they all depended for that goodness and joy on the miracle that was the work of a guest they hardly noticed. Only Mary, and the few servants who obeyed her orders knew what was happening!

This, the first of his signs, Jesus did at Cana in Galilee, and manifested his glory; and his disciples believed in him. When the disciples heard of it, saw clearly what had happened, and reflected on it, they saw in this miracle much more than water turned to wine. They saw in it a sign of his glory – of his power to bring new and glorious life into the heart of a universe where everything seems to be marked for death; his power to bring even now a blessed, healing and stabilizing influence into the personal life-situation or family problem where things are moving beyond human control into depression, collapse and divorce; his power to bring purpose and joy into a world whose celebration tends too soon otherwise to move to a sad end, and people begin to feel bored, depressed and threatened.

Now we are in a position to understand why of all the miracles which Jesus did, John attached so much importance to this first one – a miracle which did not loom so large in the minds and memories of those who wrote the other Gospels. John saw clearly that the Word became flesh, lived among us, died, and rose again, not simply to deal with individuals bringing them to salvation, blessing and healing, not simply to proclaim a noble ethic, to demand social justice, and to warn of judgement to come, but also to come again and again, here and now, into the midst of perplexing, critical and tragic human situations with his power to work the kind of renewal of which this miracle was the sign. Are we not now in a position to recognize that this was indeed only *the first* of innumerable following signs?

The message preached unashamedly from Church pulpits seventy years ago was that in spite of the Great War and the misery it had brought, in spite of the defects which were still so obvious in our social life, we could nevertheless call our society 'Christian', for there was much in our midst that was truly good, stable, and worth struggling to preserve. Everything that was worthwhile, it was then asserted, we owed to the permeating influence throught the centuries of the Christian Gospel.

Undoubtedly Paul was thinking of the influence of Christ on our secular life when in the course of writing about him he made his list of those things worth holding on to: "Finally, brethren, whatever is true, whatever is honourable, whatever is just, whatever is pure, whatever is lovely, whatever is gracious, if there is any excellence, anything worthy of praise, think about these things." (Phil. 4:8) It is a reminder that if anywhere on earth there is to be found what is truly good it is owed to the redeeming work of him who at the beginning of his ministry turned the water into wine at Cana.

Yet today even in our own land most people do not know what they owe him: "He was in the world, and the world was made through him, yet the world knew him not." (John 1:10). He is still active in the world today saving, sustaining, renewing, as he was at the wedding. The world still depends on him for its goodness. Indeed it has had so much from his generosity that it becomes absorbed in what it has, and forgets the hidden giver. P.T. Forsyth, speaking about this, quoted the saying current in the early Church: "Because of Jesus we do not seek Jesus".

The Turning Point

Though the world around us is unaware of his grace, those of us who understand it should read this story as a call to action. If we are to recover today healthy marriage and family life, and find a stable basis for worthwhile progress towards creating the good society, we must seek it from the same source. We dare not take his work among us for granted. He did this miracle for the couple and the little community at Cana because a certain woman prayed, and a few humble and concerned people gave him obedient service.

The turning point was certainly the faith and prayer of Mary. She had known all her life that he was destined to do great things for the salvation of the world he had entered, and she had waited and watched, expecting him someday to reveal who he was. She had, no doubt, heard of the happening down by the Jordan and was excited. After years of living with him she knew his concern for the little things in life which can weigh down the balance either on the side of happiness or misery. She knew that his care could reach out even to things as worldly as wine at weddings. What better place, what better occasion than he was in now to launch out on the kind of ministry she had dreamed for him?

Jesus had to try to help her to understand both her own new situation and his own. For years she had commanded him and he had obeyed her. It was her right as his mother and his duty as a son. But now that his public ministry had begun she must understand that his work was beyond her authority. His word to her was one of quiet and gentle disengagement *"O woman what have you to do with me?*" Moreover he wants her to know even now that the work into which she is trying so earnestly to press him is going to be far more costly for her and himself than she yet dreams of. The *"hour"* in which he will indeed be able to reveal himself to the world will come only after months and years of toil, trial, and waiting. When she herself is torn in heart, agonized in spirit, then will she know that his hour is come!

Yet along with this word that humbled her heart and orientated her thoughts he gave her encouragement. She had the key to the whole situation in her hand because she could go to him and pray – with confidence that he would answer.

We need to listen to Jesus' warnings about prayers that are too presumptuous, too familiar, too forgetful sometimes of what it costs God to save the world. Yet we need the encouragement and challenge which this simple incident brings to us. If we know Christ and understand how he hears and answers, we are the key people within our human situation. Around us there are friends, neighbours, relations, acquaintances facing some crisis in career or marriage, in personal stability or in choice of destiny. *"They have no wine."* They need what Christ alone can give them. If we have his ear we are surely meant to ask!

Let us not forget the *servants* who in obedience and faith carried round the water that became wine. They were privy to what was happening. They were told by Mary *"Do whatever he tells you."* There is nothing necessarily dramatic in what he so often wants us to do in the sphere of life within which he has set us. It is given its significance by the fact that he too wants to share his grace and reveal his glory through simple acts of obedient faith. "Faith and the prayers of Christians", Luther once said, "sustain the universe."

CHAPTER 6

THE CLEANSING OF THE TEMPLE

John 2:12 – 22

12 After this he went down to Capernaum, with his mother and his brothers and his disciples; and there they stayed for a few days.

13 The Passover of the Jews was at hand, and Jesus went up to Jerusalem. [14]In the temple he found those who were selling oxen and sheep and pigeons, and the money-changers at their business. [15]And making a whip of cords, he drove them all, with the sheep and oxen, out of the temple; and he poured out the coins of the money-changers and overturned their tables. [16]And he told those who sold the pigeons, "Take these things away; you shall not make my Father's house a house of trade." [17]His disciples remembered that it was written, "Zeal for thy house will consume me." [18]The Jews then said to him, "What sign have you to show us for doing this?" [19]Jesus answered them, "Destroy this temple, and in three days I will raise it up." [20]The Jews then said, "It has taken forty-six years to build this temple, and will you raise it up in three days?" [21]But he spoke of the temple of his body. [22]When therefore he was raised from the dead, his disciples remembered that he had said this; and they believed the scripture and the word which Jesus had spoken.

From Galilee to Jerusalem

When they describe how Jesus began his ministry, the other three Gospels show him entering into the conflict with Satan

42

quite directly, in the wilderness. As man, he is the second Adam, and has come to live a life of perfect obedience to God, thus reversing the disobedience of the first Adam, the shameful surrender to evil which has brought death into the world. In his temptation, decisively, at the beginning of his life he defeats the enemy who from generation to generation has held mankind in bondage, and blighted our human happiness.

John in his Gospel assumes our knowledge of this story. He reminds us, however, that Jesus, immediately his ministry on earth began, challenged the evil he had come to destroy not only in the wilderness in the presence of the angels and wild beasts, but also in the one place on earth where it was most powerfully entrenched. Jesus' first exercise of his Messianic power, as we have seen, had taken place, almost inadvertently at Cana. He retreated for a short time to think over what had happened and to plan his way ahead (v.12). Almost immediately he made the decision to go straight from Galilee to Jerusalem to begin his campaign where he knew his chief task really lay. His intention was deliberately to engage in a first dramatic and decisive encounter with the Jewish authorities in the Temple.

The Prophet Ezekiel once had the vision of a river which had its origin in a small stream of water flowing from below the threshold of a restored and cleansed Temple of God in Jerusalem. As it flowed downward and outward to other areas of the holy land around it, the volume and depth of its water increased, and its fruitfulness became more and more marvellous. Wherever it went everything teemed with new life and vegetation. Even when it entered the Dead Sea, the stagnant water became fresh. And of the trees which flourished on its banks on both sides, whose leaves had healing powers, it was written, "The leaves will not wither or their fruit fail ... because the water for them flows from the sanctuary" (Ezek. 47:12). This was the Prophet's way of stating the truth, taught everywhere in the Bible, that what prevails in the life of a community, health or sickness, happiness or misery, justice or wrongdoing, corruption or progress, depends on what people can see and hear and experience as they worship in their sanctuary.

No doubt Jesus, meditating especially on the marvellous
sign that God had given at Cana, and thinking of such
passages of Scripture, had such thoughts in his mind as he
went on his way up to Jerusalem. Here was the place from
which the river of renewal must flow outward and downward
again for God's people. Here then, was where cleansing first
of all must begin.

It was the time of the Passover feast when he made this
momentous journey. His mind must have dwelt on the Psalms
which describe the joy of such pilgrimage as well as the thrill of
arrival (Pss. 121;84). Here before him was the place where 'all
the nations' were to be taught the law of God, and to find
inspiration to beat their swords into ploughshares and their
spears into pruning hooks (Isa. 2:3 – 5). Everything here,
Zechariah had said, would be holy to the Lord, and all trading
would be banished (Zech. 14:20 – 21).

Even from a distance he must have heard the shouting of the
merchants. He made his entry where the money-changers
offering temple coinage for ordinary currency were at their
business. His reaction was immediate and violent. He had no
weapon, but the whip made out of cords was enough, since no
one present dared to withstand him in his divinely inspired
anger. There was a deliberate purpose behind the passionate
indignation which inspired his action. The prophet Malachi,
centuries before, had described the coming of the Messiah, in
the latter days, to the Temple. His oracle was now in Jesus'
mind: "The Lord whom you seek will suddenly come to his
Temple . . . But who can endure the day of his coming, and
who can stand when he appears? For he is like a refiner's
fire . . ." (Mal. 3:1 – 2). The authorities knew their
scriptures. Jesus had given them a sign which he hoped they
would fully understand.

'Zeal for thy house will consume me'

This was the disciples' first public appearance alongside their
Master. Perhaps they were nervous. We can imagine their
amazement to see him so recklessly challenge the authorities
in the full publicity of the Temple area. As they watched him
and tried to understand what was driving him on they found

themselves thinking about some verses from Psalm 69 which seemed to describe the strength and source of his emotion and to reveal his motives.

The writer of this Psalm had lived at a time of communal apostacy and disobedience to God's law when the sanctity of the Temple had been violated. He alone, refusing all compromise, had been ostracized, and even at home treated with contempt. Though he felt deep shame under the insults that were being heaped upon him, because of his holy zeal, it came to him that he ws being hated simply because the people around him hated God himself. "For zeal for thy house has consumed me, and the insults of those who insult thee have fallen on me" (v.9).

From that moment on, the disciples began to understand how always at the heart of all Jesus' passion, love, anger, as the motive of all his activity there lay this zeal for the glory of God his Father. They saw moreover that it was the key to understanding the conflict that arose between himself and his enemies. It was his pure zeal that provoked their anger as nothing else did. Perhaps the disciples sensed dimly and uncomfortably, even at this early stage in his ministry, that inevitably this zeal would literally "consume" him. At least, looking back later, they saw that they should have seen his cross looming even then. The verse of the Psalm which gripped them at that time seemed to contain a hidden prophecy of his death: *His disciples remembered that it was written, "Zeal for thy house will consume me."*

In the view of the apostles, therefore, Jesus' attack on the Jewish authorities was primarily an attack on their attitude towards God. It was directed against the cold and calculating spirit that had taken over in the religious life. They were robbing God of his honour, of their own souls, and of his reign in the hearts of the people they were meant to lead to him. Jesus' enemies reacted with such intense hatred because they felt he took God and his Word too seriously. They felt condemned and threatened by one so patently and wholly devoted to the service they themselves were guilty of neglecting. They could not tolerate such exposure.

It has become a fashion of today to interpret in quite other terms the cause of the tension which arose between Jesus and

the Jewish authorities. It is often claimed that Jesus was
crucified because he stood for the rights of the poor and
challenged an unjustly privileged and careless establishment
by identifying himself completely with the oppressed.
Undoubtedly the Bible in many of its passages shows us the
Prophet of God challenging the rulers of the day on social and
economic issues. Jesus was a Prophet and it is impossible to
deny that there was such an element in his teaching and
preaching, and that this also angered the authorities. Yet as
we read this Gospel we find nowhere the suggestion that it was
on this account that they went the length of crucifying him.
The Jesus whom we hear and encounter in the New
Testament would not have put social and economic issues
before religious issues. We cannot faithfully reflect the witness
of the New Testament by distorting its account of history.

An Enigmatic Utterance

As they looked back on that memorable first encounter
alongside Jesus with the Temple authorities, the disciples
remembered another of his utterances in the course of the
conversation – a saying the meaning of which became clear
to them only after Jesus' death and resurrection.

Sometimes a Prophet who had spoken an oracle God gave
miraculous signs to prove the truth of what had been spoken.
After Isaiah had prophesied the recovery of King Hezekiah
from a sickness, for example, we are told that the Lord made
the shadow cast by the declining sun on a sundial in the palace
turn back ten steps (Isa. 38:8). The authorities in the Temple,
angered at what they regarded as a falsely assumed air of
authority on the part of Jesus, raised the question: "*What sign
have you to show?*" Of course Jesus had already given them all
the proof of his authority that was needed. God had already
allowed him miraculously to cleanse the Temple court before
their very eyes! Yet in reply to their demand for a further sign
he made an enigmatic utterance. He spoke a Word which they
could not possibly then have understood. Yet it was meant to
haunt their minds, and to become a prophecy and a warning
to them as they remembered it. "*Destroy this temple*", he said,
"*and in three days I will raise it up.*"

When Jesus said *"Destroy this temple"* it was both a forecast of
his own violent death and also a challenge to his hearers to
fulfil the intention they were already conceiving in their hearts
and minds – the intention to destroy him. Looking on the
whole history we can see that Jesus is here in a sovereign way
actually provoking his own death at their hands (just as, later
on, he actually took command of Judas on his way to betray
him) (John 13:27). Of course he could not have expected even
his disciples to have then understood anything of what he was
saying. Yet it is printed here for us to be able to overhear it
today as the utterance of a man giving up himself in extreme
isolation of soul to the great cause which has brought him into
the world. No one around him, no one but the Father, will
understand his feelings. Yet he seems to find relief in giving
them this lonely utterance.

When they heard him speaking about raising up the
Temple in *three days* of course his enemies had no alternative
but to make the saying refer to the stone and lime of the
building before them, and they poured ridicule on him –
giving at the same time unconscious proof of how utterly
unable they were to understand the events in which they were
beginning to be involved.

In the case of the disciples of Jesus however, some time after
his death and resurrection they actually began to see how
profound and penetrating his thought had really been when he
uttered this prophecy. Indeed in the account we have here of
the incident they give us an important clue to what he then
meant: *"He spoke of the temple of his body"*, they said. They had
by this time begun to make one of the most wonderful discoveries which came to the followers of Jesus after his resurrection and ascension to heaven: That the body of Jesus, his
humanity now raised to heaven, had become the new meeting
place between God and man. The old Temple destroyed
finally by the Romans was for them already replaced by the
risen and ascended Jesus in his humanity. The phrase "the
body of Christ" is given as much prominence in the New
Testament as the Temple in Jerusalem is in the Old. What
happens in and through it, is similar to what was designed to
happen between God and his people in and through the
Temple in former times. We are reconciled to him and to one

another through his body (Eph. 2:16; Col. 1:22). We ourselves are baptized into his body (1 Cor. 12:13), become
members of it (Rom. 12, 1 Cor. 12) and partake of what he
offers us within it through the Lord's Supper (Matt. 26:26).
Jesus himself led them towards such thoughts when he spoke
of himself as the vine and of them as the branches (John 15).
The "Temple of his body" is for them now both on earth and
in heaven. It is on earth where his people are gathered in his
name to hear his word and to receive him in the bread and
wine. It is in heaven too, because he is there too. "Behold the
dwelling of God is with men. He will dwell with them, and
they shall be his people, and God himself will be with them."
(Rev. 21:3).

Zeal, Cleansing and Renewal

The disciples were not allowed by Jesus to remain mere
spectators of his zeal to cleanse. As he continued to teach them
they were often faced personally with it in his uncompro-
mising calls for purity of heart. Towards the end of his life
moreover, in the upper room, and before he gave them the
Last Supper, after a solemn action he took a basin and went
round the whole body washing the feet of each (John 13:1ff). It
was a sign of his desire to cleanse them from all the defilement
they had brought with them from the world which was going
to crucify him, and apart from which he had drawn them. In
the word he spoke to Peter who seemed for a moment to mis-
understand or resent his intention he warned them not to
resist what he was seeking to do. "If I do not wash you, you
have no part in me." There could be no renewal without
cleansing! The disciples knew themselves confronted directly
both as individuals and as a body by the same zeal for holiness
and cleansing as they had witnessed in his visit to the Temple.
     It was a lesson they never forgot and there was always a
strong conviction in the early Church that the health and
vigour of the whole community depended on its allowing itself
to be cleansed by hearing the Word and by community
discipline. They were especially concerned that people who
came to the Lord's Supper should first examine themselves

(1 Cor. 11:27 – 32) and they prayed in their liturgy to be cleansed "from all filthiness of the flesh and spirit."

We ourselves are not meant to remain spectators looking over past history when we read of the cleansing of the Temple. Jesus, as well as giving us the Lord's Supper to remind us of his desire for our renewal, has also given us the Sacrament of Baptism continually to remind us that he seeks to cleanse us as we ourselves seek to come to know him better and to receive new life from him. The picture we have of his cleansing of the Temple with its vivid details surely raises questions about the pride, commercialism and the bureaucracy which too often mars and obscures our corporate witness. The picture we have of his cleansing the disciples from the pollution of the world reminds us of his desire for each of us as individuals. The prayer of the leper can have a place in our devotions: "Lord, if you will, you can make me clean" (Matt. 8:2). Descending to details of what can clutter up our lives, a generation or two ago we heard more than we do today within the Church of the "seven deadly sins" from which we required such cleansing. Alongside of pride there was listed sloth, lust, avarice, envy, anger, gluttony. It could be a healthy exercise for us even to add such things as anxiety and gloom.

We must not, however, forget, that our cleansing is the task which Christ himself undertakes when he enlists us in his service. It is the gift he seeks to bring to us along with the new life he promises. The secret of having both is to receive him in his fullness and continually to set him before us with devotion, confidence and gratitude.

CHAPTER 7

JESUS AND NICODEMUS – I

John 2:23 – 25   3:1 – 10

23 Now when he was in Jerusalem at the Passover feast, many believed in his name when they saw his signs which he did; [24]but Jesus did not trust himself to them, [25]because he knew all men and needed no one to bear witness of man; for he himself knew what was in man.

3 Now there was a man of the Pharisees, named Nicodemus, a ruler of the Jews. [2]This man came to Jesus by night and said to him, "Rabbi, we know that you are a teacher come from God; for no one can do these signs that you do, unless God is with him." [3]Jesus answered him, "Truly, truly, I say to you, unless one is born anew, he cannot see the kingdom of God." [4]Nicodemus said to him, "How can a man be born when he is old? Can he enter a second time into his mother's womb and be born?" [5]Jesus answered, "Truly, truly, I say to you, unless one is born of water and the Spirit, he cannot enter the kingdom of God. [6]That which is born of the flesh is flesh, and that which is born of the Spirit is spirit. [7]Do not marvel that I said to you, 'You must be born anew.' [8]The wind blows where it wills, and you hear the sound of it, but you do not know whence it comes or whither it goes; so it is with every one who is born of the Spirit." [9]Nicodemus said to him, "How can this be?" [10]Jesus answered him, "Are you a teacher of Israel, and yet you do not understand this?"

An Unhappy Encounter

This chapter contains one or two of the most memorable and often-repeated sayings of Jesus. We will not, however, attempt to isolate these and analyse them apart from their immediate context. Here, as elsewhere in John's Gospel, we find that we begin to understand the force and meaning of the words used as we try to enter the dynamics of the personal encounter that is taking place between the speakers. That encounter, in this case, was an unhappy one. Nicodemus reminds us of the rich young ruler who went so eagerly to Jesus with his question about eternal life. His hopes were shattered by the word he heard, and afterwards he went away sorrowful. Nicodemus, however, in this instance went away from Jesus impatient, and possibly resentful. Some perceptive commentators point out that the mention of the "night" as the physical setting of the interview is symbolic, and helps to explain the story itself. Nicodemus comes to Jesus in the night because he belongs to the night in heart and mind. Light then begins to shine from Jesus into the darkness of his mind. But he shuts out the light in order to retain the inner darkness. He is unwilling to hear Jesus out, cuts the interview short, and leaves without ceremony, possibly while Jesus is still speaking to him. In the end he returns to the moral and spiritual darkness from which earlier he had begun to turn.

It was a miracle of grace that many months later Nicodemus did change his mind and was prepared to testify openly to his faith in Jesus. At this present stage, however, we are not given any sign of hope to relieve the tragedy of the immediate outcome.

The Background

That Nicodemus was a *"man of the Pharisees"* and a *"teacher of Israel"* indicates that he was of some importance in the city. The Pharisees were the up-to-date interpreters of Moses and the Prophets. They gave people guidance, for example, on such questions as how to know God, and how to get into his Kingdom, and about eternal life.

That he was a *"ruler of the Jews"* indicates that he was a member of the Sanhedrin, the highest ruling body of the day. He must have been associated with the Sadducees and the Priests, the Keepers of the Temple which Jesus had recently tried to cleanse.

A great 17th century Hebrew scholar commenting on the Nicodemus story quotes a legend current in early Jerusalem that a "Nicodemus ben Gurion" once held "that kind of office whose title was digger of wells, under whose peculiar care and charge was the provision of water for those who came up to the feast". It would certainly fit well into our story if the Nicodemus who came to Jesus was indeed the city engineer of his own day, responsible for maintaining the huge and abnormal water supply required for all the baptisms and lustrations which took place within the crowded city at that Passover time, and thus, even before he came to Jesus, already deeply interested in questions about baptism, water, and the Holy Spirit.

That Nicodemus was so closely bound up with such an establishment put him under great tension before he could make up his mind to visit Jesus with his questions. Nowhere did Jesus in his early ministry find such blindness to truth, or face such fierce personal opposition, as when he encountered these men to whom God had entrusted the leadership of his people. All of them had betrayed the trust God had put in them when he endowed them with their privileges. The Pharisees and Scribes had set up a tradition of their own in place of the Word of God which had come to Israel through Moses and the Prophets. They had perverted the truth to make it conform to the lies of their own minds, and they had blindly persuaded themselves that every letter of this distorted teaching had in itself divine sanctity. The Sadducees had cultivated the worst type of priestcraft to draw honour and wealth to themselves instead of God. They had become cold and calculating, had entrenched themselves in social privileges, had become an aristocracy rather than a humble priesthood. As we shall see, living within such an environment gave Nicodemus a mind-set which created almost insuperable difficulty when he confronted Jesus.

The Visit

Among so many inclined to be hostile to Jesus, what was it that impelled Nicodemus, alone as he was that night, to go to him seeking at least a friendly conversation? He may have been momentarily disturbed, indeed repelled, when he saw the fanaticism displayed by some of his colleagues in their irrational reaction to Jesus, and their immediate recourse to conspiracy against him. His own first impression of the man had been quite different from theirs. He had been struck by what he had heard of his teaching and especially of his extraordinary miracles which seemed to indicate that he had prophetic power and authority.

Moreover as he had listened to Jesus he had been struck by the contrast between what Jesus taught about the living God, so related to life and so powerful in his working, and the mass of dead doctrine associated with the schools to which he belonged. Possibly Nicodemus in this respect was dissatisfied with his own personal religious experience. No matter how faithfully he had observed the routine prescribed by the Pharisees, reality and life had been too often lacking. Might not a session with Jesus bring just that extra illumination and thrust to his own traditional teaching that would enable him to capture some of the dynamic and attractiveness of the religion of Jesus? He seemed to sense that Jesus might even help him to add to his Rabbinical store of wisdom, for he, too, obviously was a learned man.

Though he went to Jesus seeking such enrichment and counsel, he was not driven by any desperately felt need. Nicodemus was proud of his Rabbinical status and attainments. His visit was made in a mood of self-confidence. What he wanted was chiefly discussion. When he sat down before Jesus, he opened the talk with a compliment – a word of encouragement from a fellow Rabbi to this *"teacher come from God!"* He expects to be encouraged in the kind of teaching he himself was giving on the matter he was going to bring up for discussion. Perhaps, too, he flattered himself that he could bring some enlightenment to Jesus on certain aspects of the truth. It was of special interest to him that Jesus loved to discuss the very subjects he himself had for years tried to teach his own pupils, subjects such as: How does one enter the Kingdom of God and inherit eternal life?

The Tension

We are meant ourselves to be arrested by the sheer bluntness which we can overhear in Jesus' opening words to his visitor. Often when he knew that people, coming to him for help, admitted or felt some deep need, he overlooked differences and showed his unfailing compassion. We must assume therefore that he viewed Nicodemus, approaching him as he did, as a case for specially frank treatment. Jesus saw that there was such a gulf between himself and the man before him in attitude to God and life, that there could be no easy dialogue or pleasant, informative conversation between them.

He could not begin by hiding this from the man and deceiving him even for a short time about his position. His opening word to Nicodemus was therefore directed to shock him out of all self-confidence, and shatter all his illusions: *"Truly, truly I say to you, unless one is born anew, he cannot see the Kingdom of God."* Nicodemus was expected to recognize that this first word of Jesus was designed to crush out of his mind, there and then, many of the questions he had imagined himself asking as they settled down to talk.

This important word of Jesus to a man such as Nicodemus in this situation should make us uncomfortable. We may feel that it should not be given the special place among the words of Jesus which it is often accorded. We feel that our own way has been a way not of rebirth but of progress, and that we have had some success in following it. Like Nicodemus we may feel that we, too, have already had some measure of valid religious experience now and then in our lives, without any radical conversion. Surely we cannot be so far out as to deserve a word like this!

Nicodemus himself had believed that as a result of the pilgrimage he had so far made, he must be already at least on the threshold of the great hoped-for reward of all his seeking and searching: the Kingdom of God! He had known that he was not quite yet there. He had hoped that Jesus might have some encouragement to give, and some insight to share.

Instead, he heard this word: "You have not seen it, Nicodemus, far less have you come near it! Discussion, teaching, insight, effort – they will not lead you there! Only being born again! For a man rooted as you are in this world's life and establishment, there is no other way from your darkness to light!"

This, then, was Jesus' shattering announcement to his visitor: That he was indeed a blind man groping in a dark world for a truth that is not to be found by his method of searching, that the light and life of God to which he had thought himself so near, belong to another region entirely, and that the only way from the world to which he at present belonged into fellowship with Jesus was indeed by a new birth.

The Closing of the Mind

Nicodemus said to him, *"How can a man be born when he is old? Can he enter a second time into his mother's womb and be born?"*

We are free to subject this question of Nicodemus to varied interpretations. If we tend to be sympathetic with Nicodemus for instance we can hear it as expressing the wistful longing of a man who desires such rebirth but regards it as an impossible dream.

Our own view here is that an offended Nicodemus is dismissing Jesus' solemn word as brusquely as he felt Jesus himself had dealt with his polite approach to him. He intends in his reply to make a caricature of Jesus' remark, to show how ridiculous the idea of re-birth appears to his mind. There is a slightly cynical tone in the way he puts it: "How can an old man become like a foetus implanted in the womb?"

Hoskyns, in his commentary, puts the case well: "By a strange paradox, the man who has come to converse about God, and who is sure that he knows what a divine mission is, turns out to be, in spite of his delicate perceptions, a complete materialist. He can conceive of no other truth than that which has made him what he is."

An Appeal for Openness

Jesus, having effectively shocked Nicodemus, was now patient and appealing. He explained the kind of re-birth that had been in his mind. It was a complete inward renewal brought about by the Spirit of God. Nicodemus himself knew well the great Old Testament prophecy about the coming of new life to God's people which was to take place in the age-to-come – in the very Kingdom of God of which they had been speaking. It was to be a re-birth brought about through the sprinkling of water as well as by the giving of the Spirit. Jesus was no doubt referring to this passage when he spoke of being *"born of water and the Spirit"*. It is possible that he quoted it to Nicodemus: "I will sprinkle clean water upon you, and you shall be clean from all your uncleanesses . . . A new heart will I give you, and a new spirit will I put within you; and I will take out of your flesh the heart of stone and give you a heart of flesh. And I will put my spirit within you and cause you to walk in my statutes" (Ezek. 36:25 – 7).

Then an event happened which allowed Jesus suddenly to turn the conversation from Scripture to life. They may have been talking on the roof top in the cool of the evening, or they may have been in a room with windows open in the direction of the evening breeze. It came for a moment or two with some force. Jesus immediately said, "Feel it Nicodemus! The wind! Think of how far beyond your control or understanding are its movements. Can you tell where it comes from and why it chooses to come this way? Yet it is powerfully felt even though its ways are beyond your ken. You cannot understand and yet you hear and feel it! – *so it is with everyone who is born of the Spirit.*"

It was an appeal to the man before him for openness and honesty in face of all that was actually taking place in the religious world of his own day. What the wind was doing in the place where they were talking, the Spirit was doing in the hearts of men and women in contemporary Jerusalem and Judaea. We cannot doubt that Jesus had good ground for this appeal. Nicodemus had personally encountered here and there people who had come strongly under the renewing influence of the Spirit of God. The Baptist's disciples were moving around everywhere, and as well as John, Jesus' own disciples were now baptizing in Jesus' name and by his Spirit. In his words about the night wind Jesus was indeed reminding Nicodemus forcibly of what he had already observed, and

what he himself could experience if wished, – the power of
God's Spirit to bring re-birth into the lives of ordinary people.
Though he could not understand it nor analyse its workings,
*"the wind blows where it wills and you hear the sound of it, but you do
not know whence it comes or whether it goes"*.

Perhaps in this challenge to Nicodemus to become *"born of
water and the Spirit"* there was a warning to him to throw off the
fear of public opinion that had forced him to visit Jesus,
unknown to others, in the night. Nothing is given or promised
by Jesus to those who are ashamed to confess openly their
interest or their faith.

Closed Mind and Patient Teacher

The conversation between the two of them comes gradually to
an end. We have just seen how in reply to Nicodemus'
scepticism about re-birth, Jesus had pointed him to the
teaching of Scripture on the possibility of a marvellous
renewal taking place through the Spirit inwardly for anyone
who would open the heart to God; and also to the evidence of
its taking place in the contemporary world. The last word we
have from Nicodemus was a flat rejection of both the
argument and the evidence – *How can this be?*

Jesus completely rejected his plea of ignorance. His very
position at the centre of public affairs in Jerusalem as *"a teacher
of Israel"* made it impossible for him not to know what was
going on in the city and its environment! He not only accused
Nicodemus of telling a lie, but also expressed resentment at
the implication that he himself was guilty of bearing false
witness: *"We speak what we know and bear witness to what we have
seen, but you do not receive our testimony."*

Jesus, at this point slightly exasperated for a moment,
questioned whether he should continue the conversation. *"If I
have told you of earthly things and you do not believe, how can you believe
if I tell you heavenly things?"* He had much more to say. How far
was it worthwhile continuing to speak to such a man?

We believe that at this point there was an important
development in the situation. Nicodemus had not only closed
his mind, he signified that he was now ready to close the
interview. He had had enough. He had given his final word,

dismissing Jesus himself. He began even while Jesus was talking to show signs of restlessness. The account of the incident indicates that he left without ceremony even as Jesus was continuing to speak. Yet Jesus did not stop speaking. He continued to preach the Gospel to this man who had given the clearest of signs that he did not want to hear more. He went on to speak in the most appealing, profound, simple and memorable way about his Father and his own Cross. He went on in the hope that Nicodemus would overhear even as he pretended that he was otherwise engaged, and would ultimately remember what had been said. How could such words as these from Jesus ever fail to register in any mind?

We are reminded of an incidental feature in one of the Easter appearances recorded at the end of our Gospel. The disciples in the upper room had shut the door for fear of the Jews, but Jesus came, and stood in the midst, and spoke. They shut him out unwillingly, Nicodemus did it knowingly. Deliberately he decided that there was no more he need listen to, and he closed up his mind. Yet Jesus stands at the door and knocks, speaking so that his voice can be heard! We cannot make it so that he remains shut out and in silence. No matter how fully we fold up our accounts with him to file them away, he comes to re-open everything, and sometimes quite soon. "He will not fail or be discouraged" (Isa. 42:4). Even though we think we have finished with him, he is never finished with us.

CHAPTER 8

JESUS AND NICODEMUS – II
John 3:11 – 21

11 "Truly, truly I say to you, we speak of what we know, and bear witness to what we have seen; but you do not receive our testimony. [12]If I have told you earthly things and you do not believe, how can you believe if I tell you heavenly things? [13]No one has ascended into heaven but he who descended from heaven, the Son of man. [14]And as Moses lifted up the serpent in the wilderness, so must the Son of man be lifted up, [15]that whoever believes in him may have eternal life."

16 For God so loved the world that he gave his only Son, that whoever believes in him should not perish but have eternal life. [17]For God sent the Son into the world, not to condemn the world, but that the world might be saved through him. [18]He who believes in him is not condemned; he who does not believe is condemned already, because he has not believed in the name of the only Son of God. [19]And this is the judgement, that the light has come into the world, and men loved darkness rather than light, because their deeds were evil. [20]For every one who does evil hates the light, and does not come to the light, lest his deeds should be exposed. [21]But he who does what is true comes to the light, that it may be clearly seen that his deeds have been wrought in God.

From "Earthly Things" to "Heavenly Things"

Nicodemus, as we have seen, had shown himself so tough in his denial of simple facts that Jesus had misgivings about the worthwhileness of going on with the conversation. However, he felt he had not yet spoken about what mattered most in the message he had come to deliver to people like him. He therefore, contented himself with a brief expression of his exasperation as he announced his decision to go on speaking, *"If I have told you earthly things and you do not believe me, how can you believe if I tell you heavenly things?"*

What did Jesus mean when he divided what he had to speak about into "earthly things" and "heavenly things"? The meaning of these two terms, of course, becomes clear if we compare what he had already said to Nicodemus with what he actually now went on to say.

So far, Jesus, in his talk that night, had dwelt on the evidences of the impact of the Spirit of God on the earthly lives of men and women, of its power to bring about marvellous and radical change in heart, mind and attitude here and now. He had called this experience being "born again". He had even asked Nicodemus to feel the winds of the Spirit. He had deliberately taken this very down-to-earth approach because Nicodemus in making his visit had had in mind questions about such "earthly things". All this had been a good start, and Nicodemus should have responded to such an appeal to face the power of the Spirit working in his neighbourhood.

But if Jesus wanted now to go on to even better news he had to speak about God himself, about his own relationship of love to the Father as his only Son, and about why he had come into the world. Now, before he allowed Nicodemus to go, he must be made even to overhear some word about these "heavenly things". Therefore, in spite of his passing doubt whether it was worth it, he went on speaking, and we have from him this word about God so loving the world as to give his only begotten Son, about the eternal decision of love made in heaven when he himself was sent into the world, and of the quite unique heavenly nature that lay hidden in the heart of his own being even as he was speaking to this man before him.

Today we have far greater evidence around us than Nicodemus could ever have had of the *"earthly things"* – of the Spirit's power to bring re-birth and new life from above. We live after Pentecost. The Spirit of God has proved time and again within the history of the Church and in the lives of individual men and women that it is the "power of God for salvation to everyone who has faith." (Rom. 1:16). Large numbers of Christians today indeed give place at the centre of their Church life, to continual Pentecostal renewal, the cultivation of charismatic gifts, and divine healing. While we can rejoice in what is thus seen and heard today of the work of the Spirit, we must pay heed to the fact that Jesus wants continually to move the attention of our faith upwards – to the things that lie beyond the range of our earthly experience and must be grasped by faith alone.

Often he wants to lift our minds to God, the Holy Trinity, the good news of the Father and the Son and their love in the Spirit. It is when our minds and hearts are gripped by the word and vision of such "*heavenly things*" that we have a more firm and steady basis for living the Christian life and proclaiming the Christian message. John Calvin said on this subject: "Our hearts will never find calm repose till they rest on the unmerited love of God."

Before he gives his final word to Nicodemus Jesus first claims that on such matters he alone can speak with absolute certainty and authority: "*No one has ascended into heaven but he who descended from heaven, the Son of man.*" Here we are beyond the ken of the most learned Rabbi, the greatest philosopher or the most practised mystic. As one commentator puts it: "Jesus is the only one who has ever been in heaven because he comes down from heaven" (Brown). The Gospel writer himself in the Prologue has already underlined for us the sheer uniqueness of what he has to say to us on this matter: "No one has ever seen God; the only Son, who is in the bosom of the Father, he has made him known." (John 1:18).

The Earthly Way to Heavenly Things

It is a remarkable fact that even that night, Jesus, in attempting to lift Nicodemus up in mind to the level at which he could convincingly speak to him about God, felt that he had to speak about his own death. If Nicodemus was ever to know God he had to be brought to see what the Cross would reveal. It is true that at other times and on other occasions Jesus expressed his teaching about God in ways that seem more directly appealing to the human mind. We cannot forget his word to the crowd in Galilee about the Heavenly Father and his care for the sparrows and the lilies, nor his parable about the Father who waited so anxiously and longed for the prodigal son to return, and then ran and fell on his neck and kissed him. Yet here before Nicodemus he had no time for many such elaborate words. He knew, moreover, that only what was revealed in the Cross would be adequate to break down the man's stubborn resistance to the truth, in order to enable him to see and believe.

That the Cross had not yet happened did not prevent him from speaking about it there and then. It is sometimes assumed by those who interpret the Gospels that it was only late in his life that Jesus became aware that he would suffer death on the Cross. The writer of this Gospel, however, as we have seen, had no doubt that at the beginning of his ministry he knew what was going to happen to him. He knew it was bound to happen. "*So must the Son of man,*" he said, "*be lifted up.*" He knew, too, that Nicodemus was bound to be there in Jerusalem when it happened, and would be in a position to take it all in. If he could help this man to think about it properly and to see what it meant as it happened he would indeed then be able to see through to the heart of it. He wanted to tell him about it now so that then he could believe and respond!

As Jesus read the Old Testament he found that many parts of it referred to himself, his coming, and the work he was to do when he came. "You search the Scriptures," he said once to the Pharisees, "because you think that in them you have eternal life; and it is they that bear witness to me." (John 5:39) There was one remarkable story in the book of Numbers (Num. 21) which his visitor would know well, and Jesus reminded him of it, because it fitted in exactly with what he wanted to say to him about his crucifixion.

While the Israelites were passing through the wilderness on one occasion they demonstrated unbelief and disobedience. They spoke bitterly against God and Moses. While they remained in this mood a plague of serpents harassed them in their camp. Their bite was deadly and many perished. In their distress the people turned to Moses and asked him to pray for mercy. In reply to his prayer Moses was to make a fiery serpent and set it on a pole. The serpent of bronze was set up, and whenever anyone was bitten, if he looked on the bronze serpent hanging on the pole he was marvellously cured.

Through this story Jesus' own future on earth had become more clear to himself. He, too, will be "lifted up", – condemned to a brutal death. Crucifixion was the kind of death reserved by the Romans for criminals of the worst sort – painful and lingering. He will be insulted and ridiculed. He is to hang on a pole as if he himself were that serpent – mean, grovelling and spiteful. The crowd around him will be glad to see justice done, and even his friends will be tempted to imagine him a failure. He will be hanged there on that pole to bear the agony and shame alone. Often he had thought of the cry of the Psalmist out of the same kind of dereliction and isolation of the soul as he knew himself destined to face: "My God, my God why hast thou forsaken me" (Ps. 22:1). No one else can indeed be there. A work has to be done that he alone can do. A burden has to be borne that he alone can bear, and no one is able even to stand beside him as he bears it.

As he had thought it over Jesus had found his mind arrested by another dark aspect of the story. He found that it described to him not only the kind of death that awaited him, but the kind of community that was going to inflict it on him. Already in Jerusalem he had faced the deadly and devilish antagonism of the kind of people who had this world's life under their leadership. He knew that as time passed he would experience the same falsehood, bitterness against God, and hatred of opposition everywhere. He knew that his death was going to be the scene of the worst and most shameful outbreak of malice and injustice the world had ever witnessed. At the beginning of his interview with Nicodemus he had dwelt on the blindness and darkness of our natural human condition – on our need for light and life. Now in speaking of this story he dwells on the deadly poison that has entered the human blood, on our viciousness of mind and heart, and on our need to be reconciled to the God we have rejected with such proud enmity.

However grim and dark its hints of our human condition, however, Jesus recalls the story so as to preach not condemnation but salvation. He underlines the power of his

Cross and the transformation it can bring wherever its
influence is allowed to work freely. One believing look will
bring healing to whomever turns towards it. Nothing else is
demanded – nothing in the hand, no other sacrifice than
what has been made by Jesus himself, only a look by a poor
soul seeking mercy, and driven perhaps by sheer despair! One
look, and everything is changed. There is hope, health,
freedom, and eternal life.

'God so loved . . .'

The Cross is called the "wondrous Cross" because when
people behold it they see God. Jesus could have spoken about
what it cost himself to come into this bitter poisoned perishing
world. We sing about it at Christmas:

> "Sacred Infant, all Divine
> What a tender love was thine,
> Thus to come from highest bliss
> Down to such a world as this."

How greatly he loved us! Yet here he prefers to speak to us
about how greatly the Father loved us in giving *"his only-
begotten Son"*.

H.R. Mackintosh in one of his lectures had a story of the
captain of an Aberdeen trawler who had his only son on the
bridge of his boat in the North Sea when a completely
unexpected enormous wave washed the deck and swept the
boy away before his own eyes. Later on, still horror struck and
awed at what had happened, he told one of the leading Pastors
in the city that never till that moment had he had the faintest
conception of what it cost God to send Christ into the world.

We can find in the writings of each New Testament Apostle
some new rich insight into the meaning and message of what
happened at Calvary. Here we have the most important and
essential thing said about that message, a word from Jesus
himself about its revelation of a sacrifice that was made in
heaven out of the fullness, uncalculating tenderness and grace
of the Father's love.

Look at it! In comparison, our human love is hopelessly
faint and poor, for it has so often to be kindled and stirred by

the worth of what it goes out towards. Indeed we sometimes love only when we see something worth gaining. But here in this divine love we see a fountain full in itself and flowing freely in the sheer self-giving grace. No worth in us to kindle a spark of it! Paul reminds us that it was "when we were yet sinners", indeed, "when we were enemies" (Rom. 5:8, 10) that God sent his Son to die for us.

There is no prior calculation of whether anything might be given back in return. No cost too great! He pays without heed everything it takes to deliver us and bring us back. He had only one son, and he sent him! When I read John 3:16 I cannot help thinking of one Old Testament passage, of the place where God tells Abraham to offer Isaac as a sacrifice on the mountain. "Take now thy son, thine only son Isaac whom you love and offer him." Where does it come from, the tenderness of feeling that throbs through that word to Abraham, if not from the heart that has faced up beforehand to the cost of making such a sacrifice? He knows even then as he seeks the foreshadowings of his own coming sacrifice, that Isaac will be spared because his own dear one will be given.

It is sometimes imagined that the chief barrier against the consummation of our forgiveness is in our own minds, alienated from God, full of suspicion and bitterness. The Cross is therefore held to be simply a dramatic display aimed to demonstrate the extent to which his love is prepared to go in order to win us back. The barrier to our redemption, however, was in our whole situation. We were perishing, helpless, and doomed, as well as estranged in mind and heart. We had become the victims of overwhelming destructive power. In the Cross, God offers the sacrifice. He resigned himself to whatever it cost in pain and effort to rescue us. He sent his Son to abandon himself to our state and fate, to rescue us from our eternal doom.

And now the great inward miracle or reconciliation to God can begin to happen within us. Strangely, when we read the story of Christ's passion and Cross we are constrained to feel our part in it, and our own responsibility for it. Our own sin is truly uncovered. We see what we ourselves have involved him in, with all our waywardness, carelessness, and vice. Whatever our sin may have done to other men and women, now we see that it was directed also at God himself in this man who has so loved us! This is why when we really look and see what he has suffered from us we begin to change. We experience true repentance. The hatred which we begin to see we have shown to God we find is now redirected at ourselves – not to become an inwardly damaging repression, but a healing self-denial that can deliver us for ever, if we will to have it, from pride and sloth, from lust and unbelief, and enable us to walk in newness of life.

CHAPTER 9

THE BAPTIST – THE FINAL TESTIMONY
John 3:22 – 36

22 After this Jesus and his disciples went into the land of Judea; there he remained with them and baptized. [23]John also was baptizing at Aenon near Salim, because there was much water there; and people came and were baptized. [24]For John had not yet been put in prison.

25 Now a discussion arose between John's disciples and a Jew over purifying. [26]And they came to John, and said to him, "Rabbi, he who was with you beyond the Jordan, to whom you bore witness, here he is, baptizing, and all are going to him." [27]John answered, "No one can receive anything except what is given him from heaven. [28]You yourselves bear me witness, that I said, I am not the Christ, but I have been sent before him. [29]He who has the bride is the bridegroom; the friend of the bridegroom, who stands and hears him, rejoices greatly at the bridegroom's voice; therefore this joy of mine is now full. [30]He must increase, but I must decrease."

31 He who comes from above is above all; he who is of the earth belongs to the earth, and of the earth he speaks; he who comes from heaven is above all. [32]He bears witness to what he has seen and heard, yet no one receives his testimony; [33]he who receives his testimony sets his seal to this, that God is true. [34]For he whom God has sent utters the words of God, for it is not by measure that he gives the Spirit; [35]the Father loves the Son, and has given all things into his hand. [36]He who believes in the Son has eternal life; he who does not obey the Son shall not see life, but the wrath of God rests upon him.

A Prophet in Eclipse

John the Baptist after his experience at the Baptism of Jesus continued his ministry. The revelation that Jesus was the Messiah encouraged him to be all the more zealous in proclaiming that the Kingdom was indeed "at hand". He still demanded that as people repented they should be baptized with water. He bore witness to Jesus as the one who would baptize with the Spirit.

For Jesus too the message was the same as John's: "Repent: for the Kingdom of God is at hand." (Matt. 4:17). Like John, he must have felt that Baptism was a sign that could help people to renounce the present age and the self-life, and to cleanse themselves from the evil of their past ways. He taught his own disciples also to baptize as John did. Thus for some time before John was put in prison, an observer could find Jesus in one part of the country and John in another, both preaching what seemed to be a similar message, and both encouraging Baptism.

Naturally since other sects, flourishing at the time, had rites of purification which looked like Baptism, there was much confusion in people's minds about such movements and rites. We do not wonder then that a *discussion arose between John's disciples and a Jew over purifying*. It was natural also that comparisons should be made. It was obvious that the older man's ministry was on the wane, and someone brought to him the report that Jesus was not far away baptizing people and *"all are going to him!"*

There is not a trace of envy in John's reply: *"No one can receive anything except what is given him from heaven."* It reveals him full of gratitude. He himself in his day has received so much to pass on to others! He is grateful for his call to preach, for the answers to his hopes and prayers for the coming of the Messiah, for the new insights and visions given to him at the Jordan, for the gifts that have enabled him to make his witness clear to others. His ministry has so far been crowned with success. Facing his own inevitable decline his mood is of prayerful and confident resignation – especially since he is being eclipsed by Jesus for the sake of whose glory he has hitherto lived his whole life.

Luther, at this point in the Gospel, compared the attitude and ministry of John with that of the Roman clergy of his day, and he described this utterance of the Baptist as 'golden text'. The bishops and priests of Rome, he affirmed, taught, preached and exercised authority according to earthly tradition without ever seeking inspiration and guidance from heaven – from a living Word of God. They did not seek their calling or position from heaven, and pushed, schemed or worked to obtain their offices. Luther pled for a ministry that looks upwards for its inspiration, gifts and preferments.

Of course much that we have to pass on to each other within the Church we receive from below. Each of us in the laity has quite natural talents and abilities which we can put to good use in helping others within the body of Christ and enriching its community life and worship. Teachers and preachers in the ordained ministry can pass on the wisdom and understanding that has come to them through training, through good theological writing, and libraries of commentaries. All this from below! All this is good in its place.

The New Testament elsewhere encourages us to look where John the Baptist directed us. It is to the ascended Christ who, knowing what we need within the Church, pours out upon us from above a multitude of different gifts so that one may help and encourage another by sharing what has thus been given, and so that in this way the Church may be built up and its life enriched (cf. Eph. 4:8 – 13). He continually calls and equips some to be pastors, teachers and leaders. He seeks continually to open from above both the scriptures and the human understanding, that a fresh and relevant Word may continually be heard (Luke 24:vv.27, 45). Moreover the love and the patience which can enable us to devote ourselves to the Church, to each other, and to the world around us, can be received only in the same way, as the greatest gift of all, coming to us continually from above.

The "Friend of the Bridegroom"

We have already pointed out (see p.16) that his contact and conversation with Jesus brought to the mind of John the Baptist some aspects of the Old Testament message that he had hitherto missed in his preaching about the coming Messiah. This present passage which gives us John's final word about Jesus shows us that as time went on he was able to discover even more fully what the Old Testament said about the Christ and, indeed, about himself.

When the prophets described the relationship of God to his people they sometimes used the analogy of the love, hope and trust involved in betrothal and marriage. God was the husband who had loved and wooed his bride Israel. They likened the sin of Israel to the adultery of an unfaithful wife who soon after the happy first days of wedlock, gives herself up to playing the harlot. This does not alter the resolve of God's love. He goes through the agony of a great forgiveness, and with infinite patience waits and woos back his bride with an ardour even greater, because it is more costly, than that which won her in the first place.

It seemed to John that the Old Testament passages which referred to this aspect of God's love for his people were at the same time valid descriptions of the ardour and faithfulness which he saw now being demonstrated by Jesus in seeking to draw people with his friendship. His approach to human souls was like that of a bridegroom seeking to win their complete confidence and trust so that they could now enter a relationship of love, warm, deep and inviolate. Jesus confirmed all these thoughts of himself when he likened his offer of the Kingdom to an invitation to a wedding feast.

In the light of such thoughts John had begun to understand in a new way the place he himself had been given in God's plan to win the world. He had been given the task of the "Friend of the Bridegroom". He had to act as a messenger for the bridegroom, to procure and prepare the bride for his coming, and of course it was his privilege to share even intimately in the thrill and joy of the moment when the voice of the Bridegroom was heard announcing his arrival. John confesses here that he had shared that joy to the full as he had stood by and watched Jesus seeming to take his own place at the centre of the movement he had initiated.

There is indeed a suggestion here that John himself had had opportunities of hearing Jesus' own preaching to the crowds around him and that he had had such joy confirmed by the very tone of Jesus' own voice as he had appealed to people to respond to himself.

"*This joy of mine is now full,*" he could honestly say when the stranger came and told him that people were leaving him and going to Jesus. He had never imagined any other outcome of his ministry. The Bride belonged to the Bridegroom. He found joy in the fact that he was no longer needed. It is in this context that John uttered his memorable words: "*He must increase, but I must decrease.*" We have admired the selflessness of this man. Here he takes us to the heart of it, and gives us the secret. It comes without being cultivated or thought about, to those who allow themselves to become absorbed as John did, in the glory and wonder of what is happening around us in the presence of The Christ.

A Final Testimony

The closing verses of this chapter are a tribute to Jesus. On first reading they seem to be a parenthesis in which the writer of the Gospel interrupts the narrative and gives us his own reflections. Some critics suggest that the Gospel author is here reflecting on the contrast between Nicodemus and John the Baptist.

We ourselves, however, feel it more likely that this whole passage is the continuation and the conclusion of the Baptist's own testimony to Jesus, and reflects his developing thought about his friend, the Messiah. When he made this utterance John had possibly overheard from others more about the teaching of Jesus and had seen more clearly the course his ministry was going to follow. The difficult phrase, "*No one receives his testimony,*" may simply express his perplexity over a growing opposition to Jesus appearing here and there at that time. He is appealing to his contemporaries to listen not to himself, for he had had only a limited measure of the Spirit, but to Jesus on whom God had set such a final seal, and whose every word was a Word of God. (v.34) In closing he repeats what he has already said in the witness he gave at the Baptism of Jesus (v.35), and his final verse is an appeal to his generation to choose the "*eternal life*" offered through faith in him, in face of the certainty that otherwise they will remain under "*the wrath of God*".

CHAPTER 10

THE WOMAN OF SAMARIA – I
John 4: 1 – 26

4 Now when the Lord knew the Pharisees had heard that Jesus was making and baptizing more disciples than John ²(although Jesus himself did not baptize, but only his disciples), ³he left Judea and departed again to Galilee. ⁴He had to pass through Samaria. ⁵So he came to a city of Samaria, called Sychar, near the field that Jacob gave to his son Joseph. ⁶Jacob's well was there, and so Jesus, wearied as he was with his journey, sat down beside the well. It was about the sixth hour.

7 There came a woman of Samaria to draw water. Jesus said to her, "Give me a drink." ⁸For his disciples had gone away into the city to buy food. ⁹The Samaritan woman said to him, "How is it that you, a Jew, ask a drink of me, a woman of Samaria?" For Jews have no dealings with Samaritans. ¹⁰Jesus answered her, "If you knew the gift of God, and who it is that is saying to you, 'Give me a drink,' you would have asked him, and he would have given you living water." ¹¹The woman said to him, "Sir, you have nothing to draw with, and the well is deep; where do you get that living water? ¹²Are you greater than our father Jacob, who gave us the well, and drank from it himself, and his sons, and his cattle?" ¹³Jesus said to her, "Every one who drinks of this water will thirst again, ¹⁴but whoever drinks of the water that I shall give him will never thirst; the water that I shall give him will become in him a spring of water welling up to eternal life." ¹⁵The woman said to him, "Sir, give me this water, that I may not thirst, nor come here to draw,"

16 Jesus said to her, "Go, call your husband, and

72

come here." [17]The woman answered him, "I have no husband." Jesus said to her, "You are right in saying, 'I have no husband'; [18]for you have had five husbands, and he whom you now have is not your husband; this you said truly." [19]The woman said to him, "Sir, I perceive that you are a prophet. [20]Our fathers worshipped on this mountain; and you say that in Jerusalem is the place where men ought to worship." [21]Jesus said to her, "Woman, believe me, the hour is coming when neither on this mountain nor in Jerusalem will you worship the Father. [22]You worship what you do not know; we worship what we know, for salvation is from the Jews. [23]But the hour is coming, and now is, when the true worshipers will worship the Father in spirit and truth, for such the Father seeks to worship him. [24]God is spirit, and those who worship him must worship in spirit and truth." [25]The woman said to him, "I know that Messiah is coming (he who is called Christ); when he comes, he will show us all things." [26]Jesus said to her, "I who speak to you am he."

Encounter by the Well

Weary, thirsty, and hungry when he arrived at the well at Samaria in an intense heat, Jesus sent his disciples to the nearby village for food. He had originally intended to take another, more usual, way on his journey from Jerusalem to the North, but an inner impulse had directed him to this longer and more tiring route: *He had to pass through Samaria.* When the woman arrived, he knew that his Father had providentially led him. He had to speak to her. What took place between Jesus and herself contrasts sharply with what we have just witnessed in the interview between Jesus and Nicodemus. The latter, coming by night, and wanting to be friendly, took the initiative and approached Jesus confidently, only finally to become tight-lipped and obstinate. She on the other hand, coming to him in blazing daylight, was at the beginning full of suspicion, even hostility. The talking began on the initiative of Jesus, and only later did she open up and reveal herself.

She reveals herself to us engagingly as she talks on and on.
We discover that she was hightly intelligent and well educated
in the history and tradition of her nation and village. She was
interested in religion and was prepared quickly to take up a
theological point and talk it through. She belonged to a
religious community looking for a Messiah whom they
believed their Scriptures promised them.

As the conversation develops, we gradually find out what
Jesus began to discern as he talked with her. She was living in
her village with a man who was not her husband. This
accounted for her being there at the well when the heat was so
intense that no one else was about. She had wanted to be there
alone, for she had felt herself to be an outcast, embarrassed
when she had to mix with people who might think her a bad
influence, whisper to one another, and perhaps register their
disapproval of her presence.

Though her approach and response contrasted so sharply
with those of Nicodemus, Jesus' aim in speaking to both was
the same, and his conversation followed the same pattern of
thought. He began by talking of "earthly things" and then
moved to "heavenly things" (cf. pp.59ff.). We find here in the
case of this woman that his desire throughout is to present
himself as the Messiah, the Son of God who has sought her out
and come to meet her where she is, at this well. He wants to
raise her mind finally to the spiritual nature of God the Father
who in response to his seeking love wants her true and loving
worship and devotion. But, as with Nicodemus, he tries first
to win her through talk that is on a more earthly level. He
shows his human understanding of the burden she is
needlessly bearing, and of the dissatisfaction he feels in the
way she is living. He speaks of the marvellous change and
renewal that can take place in those who receive what he can
here and now give.

"Give me a drink"

Everything began unpromisingly. The etiquette of decency
which prevailed in those days would have prevented a woman
from opening up the conversation had she even desired to do
so. It was therefore Jesus, more keen to open talk than to

obtain any favour from her, who broke the silence and said *"Give me a drink"*.

It was an opportunity for her to insult him, and she took it. Here was a Jew! Typical of most Samaritan women of those days she hated the Jews – and all the more so because she knew they despised Samaritans. Here, moreover, was a man! Her life experience had made her slightly bitter and cynical towards the opposite sex. That she had had five husbands before she began to live with her present partner seems to indicate that she had been through more than one divorce. She felt that Jesus with his request, *"Give me a drink"*, had given her at least a moment of power over him, and she tried to wound him even as she made a show of helping him. Jesus, before he was offered a drink was therefore given a taste of the backlash of years of anti-Jewish cultural training given in home and perhaps school in Samaria, and he was made to feel the personal frustration of a very unhappy individual: *"How is it that you, a Jew, ask a drink of me, a woman of Samaria?"* Her voice rang with contempt – the Jewish male snob, condescending to take notice of her existence only because she happened to have a pitcher handy when he was desperately in need of it! She well knew that in Jerusalem she would not be given a place even among the beggars in the street.

Here we are forced to take notice of the deepening humiliation to which as time passed the Son of God was subjected when he dwelt amongst us in order to save us.

Here in the eyes of one he has come to save he is regarded as belonging to a hated race of men. He sits at the side of a well and begs a drink of a passer-by. In the end we will be asked to behold the same man (John 19:5) crying out I "thirst" as exhausted and broken, scorned and ridiculed, he dies (John 19:28).

"Look again and ask!"

Jesus felt the insult and was grieved at her aloofness. He was well used to such treatment. Many around him seemed to have neither the eye nor the ear for anything other than the superficial, and he had little of that to offer. Yet he had been sent here by the Father to meet her, to reveal his love and to liberate her.

He expressed his hope that she would think again, as he appealed to her with a second request *"If you knew the gift of God, and who it is that is saying to you, 'Give me a drink', you would have asked him, and he would have given you living water"*. Obviously his concern is to persuade her to ask for what he has come to give her. If only she could overcome the racism, the class distinction and sexism that were reinforcing her natural blindness; if only she were given the insight to penetrate behind his lowly Jewish appearance to see who it was, there speaking to her; if only she would listen, look, and believe; she would find herself beginning now to ask!

We have to note how skilfully he phrased his appeal, obviously choosing his words carefully. He offered her *"living water"*.

He hoped that this phrase could at least be taken as an expression of his sympathy for her as she prepared to fill her already heavy jar with much heavier water. She was a clever and intelligent woman, and this was the task to which her place in life and especially her sex condemned her – day after day! – this intolerable dead weight of stone and water! It had seemed at times to be a symbol, too, of her domestic slavery in the kitchen in the service of a man not worth it. Perhaps here was a different type of man, now speaking to her, who really understood her mood, and her lot in life?

Jesus had a further purpose in the phrase he chose for his offer to her. He knew that the woman to whom he was speaking was ready to respond to talk about God. No matter how far she had failed to live up to it, she knew well what the phrase *"living water"* meant in religious tradition, even in Samaria. It stood for the joyful and satisfying experience of refreshment and new life that the souls of sincere believers received when they entered communion with God, who was himself the "fountain of living water". He hoped his offer would awaken within her something of this thirst for the living God that she had heard about from the days of her youth.

She was certainly touched and attracted by his sympathy and understanding of her feelings, and indeed he seems also to have begun to awaken desires within her for a better way of life. She felt he would not be able to speak as convincingly as he did, unless there was something genuine behind his offer, yet she was obviously confused about what he was really offering to do for her. *"Sir"* she said, *"you have nothing to draw with, and the well is deep; where do you get that living water? Are you greater than our father Jacob, who gave us the well, and drank from it himself, and his sons, and his cattle?"* Two things are clear: she is interested in him, and in what he has to offer, and she wants now to remain in his company and hear more of what he has to say about himself.

The Word Reveals his Glory

It is well known that the Gospel of John makes much of the seven miraculous signs which the Evangelist especially selects to show how in and through them Jesus manifested his glory. Alongside such signs, the Gospel also at times give prominence to certain words uttered when Jesus becomes specially majestic in his speaking – words that are no less inspired or eloquent in revealing his serene power and divine self-confidence than any miracle could be. This woman now needs no further argument, nor does she need any sign. She is ready to listen, to ask, and to receive, and Jesus is inspired to put everything he has to say and give to her into such a spoken word.

As we ourselves listen to him speaking it, we are reminded of the great final appeal spoken in the name of God by a Prophet in Babylon to captive Israel just as they were about to be released by God from their captivity. Though a great and exciting opportunity for freedom was before them, some of them were loath to take it. They had begun to settle down comfortably in their foreign homes, amidst the wealth and culture which Babylon now offered them. The Prophet in the name of God tried to expose the emptiness of it all compared with what God was now holding before them: "Ho, everyone who thirsts, come to the waters; and he who has no money, come, buy and eat. Come, buy wine and milk without money and without price. Why do you spend your money for that which is not bread and your labour for that which does not satisfy? Hearken diligently to me, and eat what is good, and delight yourselves in fatness." (Isaiah 55:1 – 2). Jesus, as was often his custom, put himself both in the place of the Prophet

and in the place of God, and to the poor deluded, captive soul
before him, gave fresh expression to the Word that had been
spoken.

> "*Everyone who drinks of this water shall thirst again, but
> whoever drinks of the water that I shall give him will
> never thirst; the water that I shall give him will become in
> him a spring of water welling up to eternal life.*"

Here alone is what satisfies and lasts while nothing else
endures! Here is a treasure incomparable and irreplaceable!
Jesus puts himself in a class by himself over against the whole
world at its best. He promises to transform the way she lives
and the attitudes she takes in life. He promises her a new task
and a new sphere of influence. No longer will she remain the
social drudge, in bondage to the house and the kitchen and
the bed. She will now become the centre of a great renewing
influence on other lives around her. His words glow with
warmth as he speaks them, and she cannot but listen. He
makes her want what he is promising, and certain of what
he is offering – certain too that all he is waiting for is her
own decision to ask. Therefore she begins to do so: "*Sir, give
me this water, that I may not thirst, nor come here to draw!*" She is
so certain of his power to put her *whole* life right, that in her
prayer she makes him responsible for delivering her from her
physical drudgery, as well as for responding to the intense
longing of her thirsty soul for the living God. Of course these
unforgettable words of Jesus were intended not for the
woman only, but for all of us today. They were meant to be
re-echoed to awaken each generation to its need, to bring the
grace they promise to whoever hears and asks in any age.
They never seem to belong to the past, as we hear them
again and again, and they will never do so. They are meant
to make us, too, want what he has to give. We are cold
indeed, and distant from reality if they do not reach and
touch us deeply. They come to us as the perfect expression
of who he is, and of what he has come to do for each and all
of us.

The Moment of Truth

Her prayer "*Sir, give me this water, that I may not thirst, nor come here to draw,*" expressed sincerely the desire of her heart and mind, but it revealed that she was still confused about what he was really offering her. Her confusion was possibly due to her uncertainty about herself. She had one step more to go before things could become quite clear.

In the presence of Jesus she had become uncomfortably conscious that her life had been sinful as well as empty. But she had not yet been entirely honest and frank with him. There could be no possibility of her receiving new life without forgiveness, and that meant complete openness before him. The moment of truth had to come. He decided mercifully that he could bring it about better than she herself could, and in his grace he did it for her, quickly, abruptly and thoroughly: "*Go, call your husband, and come here*". *The woman answered him, "I have no husband". Jesus said to her, "You are right in saying 'I have no husband'; for you have had five husbands, and he whom you now have is not your husband; this you said truly*".

He did it skilfully, and with infinite tact. He made no prior demand for confession. He did not even first explain why it had to be made. All that would have prolonged the agony. In his very accusation, he worded for her the confession she already wanted to make. One step in the revelation gently led into another. She was hurt badly as it all came out, and she felt it, even though by then she knew that he had already known it. Being deeply ashamed before him because of the very self-respect he had already given her, she tried immediately if possible to change the subject. She began to talk theology (which is the best way at times to get off the most uncomfortable challenge of God himself) and with infinitely gracious understanding of her motives and feelings he let the whole matter drop, and allowed her to recover her composure. The clear confession he had made on her behalf was enough: "If we confess our sins, he is faithful and just, and will forgive our sins and cleanse us from all unrighteousness (1 John 1:9).

What he did for her was thorough. The light he so suddenly and clearly shone on the festering sore that had caused her so much of her misery, brought immediate relief and the promise of health. When she later spoke of what had happened to her that day she always spoke of the relief and joy that flooded into her life at the very moment he uncovered her sins through the light of his love and holiness. It was divine miracle! It takes us back to the message spoken so eloquently in the picturesque language of the thirty-second Psalm. The Psalmist first speaks of the misery of unconfessed sin: "When I declared not my sin, my body wasted away through my groaning all the day long." Then he speaks of the great moment of release when "I said 'I will confess my transgressions to the Lord'". The rest of the poem dwells with joy on the blessedness and confidence of those whose sin has now been so completely and simply dealt with. Having been exposed it is now gone for ever! "Be glad in the Lord and shout for joy, all you upright in heart!"

Preparation for Witness

He knows she will want to become a witness to what has happened and she will want like the Psalmist to speak of this new and decisive experience: "*Come, see a man who told me all that I ever did!*"

His concern is to give her more to speak about than simply what has happened to herself, and to anchor her faith on more than one sudden experience, even though it had brought such joy and liberation. Therefore he holds her there in order to teach her about himself and God the Father. She herself is encouraged to lead the discussion on. She had felt that, by exposing her sin as he had done, he must at least be a Prophet. From the thought of his being the Prophet her mind rambled on to one of chief concerns of the Prophets – that of worship. She asked his opinion on where one found the best form of worship. He gave her his views, and it was to her that Jesus spoke his words: "*God is spirit, and those who worship him must worship in spirit and truth*". One of his chief concerns now was to help her to understand the source of the seeking love that had led him to the well that day to find her. It was because *the Father seeks* such worship that he himself had come into the world to win it from men and women, and here he was now seeking it from her! Following such an appeal she is led to talk about the

Messiah who, she believed, *"will show us all things"*. It was a simple matter for Jesus who had already shown her so much, to bring everything to a climax: *"I who speak to you am he"*. She was certain now that he was no other than the Christ.

It was talk free, open, intelligent. Jesus encouraged her to express herself on her own level and sought then to lift the talk to his level. He even seized an opportunity to defend his race against the anti-semitism she had previously shown – *"Salvation is from the Jews"*, he reminded her.

We do not wonder that, thrilled with her new discoveries, as well as liberated from her burden, *she left her water jar*, and went away into the city with her message. That she left the jar was a sign of radical change in the whole course of her life. She was now free from what it stood for. She had left the man for whom she had filled it. She had left her sin, and her bondage.

CHAPTER 11

THE WOMAN OF SAMARIA – II
John 4: 27 – 42

27 Just then his disciples came. They marvelled that he was talking with a woman, but none said, "What do you wish?" or, "Why are you talking with her?" [28]So the woman left her water jar, and went away into the city, and said to the people, [29]"Come, see a man who told me all that I ever did. Can this be the Christ?" [30]They went out of the city and were coming to him.

31 Meanwhile the disciples besought him, saying, "Rabbi, eat." [32]But he said to them, "I have food to eat of which you do not know." [33]So the disciples said to one another, "Has any one brought him food?" [34]Jesus said to them, "My food is to do the will of him who sent me, and to accomplish his work. [35]Do you not say, 'There are yet four months, then comes the harvest?' I tell you, lift up your eyes, and see how the fields are already white for harvest. [36]He who reaps receives wages, and gathers fruit for eternal life, so that sower and reaper may rejoice together. [37]For here the saying holds true, 'One sows and the other reaps'. [38]I sent you to reap that for which you did not labour; others have laboured, and you have entered into their labour."

39 Many Samaritans from that city believed in him because of the woman's testimony, "He told me all that I ever did." [40]So when the Samaritans came to him, they asked him to stay with them; and he stayed there two days. [41]And many more believed because of his word. [42]They said to the woman, "It is no longer because of your words that we believe, for we have heard for ourselves, and we know that this is indeed the Saviour of the world."

A Shared Joy

The woman was thrilled and radiant. Talking with Jesus had changed everything. She had met the Christ, the Saviour of the world. He had broken into her isolation and self-centredness, and had given her inward liberation and joy. He had led her into touch with the seeking love of God the Father.

The experience of the day had filled Jesus, too, with joy. In Jerusalem recently he had found himself in alien surroundings engaged in a work that seemed fruitless. Even amongst the crowds which had come round with enthusiasm he had found too many who wanted to see miracles, rather than to hear and respond to his message. He had found himself growing suspicious when people like Nicodemus made approaches to him.

In the midst of so much uncertainty about the ultimate worthwhileness of some of his efforts at ministry, however, here before him now was clear evidence that a work that promised to be more fruitful was beginning to take place. He himself had been given the task of bringing it to perfection. He was thrilled to be here, as he said to *accomplish* what he felt was a great work of God (v.34).

He was thankful that the task before him was pleasant and indeed joyful. He was to be given the privilege of reaping where *others have laboured*. Possibly a local priest or some godly community leaders had spent years in patient teaching, in prayer and pastoral care, amongst this people and after years of nurture and waiting everything was ready for a great community renewal.

Here they were coming across the fields towards him, a whole village, thirsty and searching souls ready to open their lives to his influence as the woman had already done. He looked forward to many miracles greater than the works that had already astonished Galilee and Jerusalem. He was going to reap the kind of harvest rejoiced in by the angels in heaven. Men and women were going to find God for now and for eternity.

He was looking forward especially to the work, joy and satisfaction of dealing intimately with individuals. He had come to found a Kingdom, and to build a Church. He had a message for nations and governments about their social structures. But he never lost sight of the one among the many. Groups, congregations, cities were made up of individuals each designed for a special place within a community; each with his or her own name, each his or her own background, desires, and needs; each made for a special place within God's heart and mind and purpose.

What had brought Jesus into the world was not only the desire to restore a fallen universe and to acclaim a universal triumph over evil, but also what a great preacher of a former generation described as a "passion for souls". Each around him had become lost, each following his or her own way. Each had to be sought and found in his or her own place, and won as this woman had been, through personal understanding and love.

A Revealing Intrusion

He was therefore deeply disappointed to discover the attitude which his disciples took up when they arrived on the scene. Of course he had been keen to involve them in this work. He had hoped to be able to teach them how to face, in their own future work, other situations of the same kind as this village presented. He had looked forward eagerly to their arrival, but they failed to respond either to the situation or to his own personal feelings. What had thrilled him they found strange. They soon revealed how much they were out of sympathy. *They marvelled that he was talking with a woman* – embarrassed at least, if not a little shocked! Did he not clearly see the kind of woman she was – alone there – and so forward?

The story suggests that out of a desire to save him from his mistake their first instinct was to go and immediately interrupt him, but no one was able to pluck up the courage to do it. *None said, "What do you wish?" or "Why are you talking with her?"* (Some preachers have sarcastically suggested that when they overheard bits of the theological conversation, and discovered the brilliance of the woman's mind, they became too ashamed to expose their own ignorance.)

Finally their insensitivity to Jesus' feelings came out clearly when they pressed him to eat. It was he who had sent them to buy food because he had been so hungry. But now the joy he felt in his heart and soul had made him forget his hunger and had indeed banished all thought of his physical needs. He could not be bothered at the moment to return to such a mundane concern as lunch. Could they not understand that this thrilling experience of harvesting in the Kingdom of God had simply taken away for the time being his earthly hunger and thirst? The disciples however could not even imagine any such transforming uplift of heart and mind to be possible, and they decided that someone else had given him something.

Of course we are meant to notice the contrast, between the woman and the disciples shown so skilfully by the narrator in telling the story. She forgets her waterpot because she has found so much else to satisfy the soul. They, unaware of what there is to thrill anyone, can think of nothing else but lunch!

The Reproach

Jesus immediately reproached them for their short-sightedness. He questioned their outlook and attitude, and showed them where they had gone wrong. He accused them of forgetting some of his instructions to them when he had originally ordained them, and sent them out to serve him, and also of neglecting an important aspect of the task he had given them in the world.

They had come to regard that task as primarily and diligently to sow the good seed of the Gospel here and there in the world around them as far and wide as possible wherever they could find people listening. They had taken to heart Jesus' teaching in the parables about the sowing of the good seed of the Kingdom and its growth where it was received. They had retold his stories. They had spoken about his miracles. They had shown how new and different were his moral standards from those accepted by the world or the Pharisees. They had repeated his calls to repent and had underlined the moral and social challenge of his message. They had believed that through such hard work such diligent sowing of the good seed, eventually the harvest would come. But they had not thought too much about the reaping that had to follow the sowing if the crop was finally to be gathered.

They had coined a slogan: *"yet four months, then comes the harvest"*. They would leave all that to others and to the future. Perhaps the harvest would look after itself!

It was on this very point that Jesus challenged them. He rebuked them for their continual repetition of the *"yet four months"* slogan. He reminded them that when he had sent them out he had spoken to them explicitly about the need to reap the harvest as well as to sow the seed: *"I sent you to reap."* His concern was therefore now to recall them to this whole neglected dimension of their ministry. He had not sent them out as pioneers of a new faith. All round them wherever they went they could have discovered that *others have laboured* in the fields to which they were being sent. Here and there some seed had already taken deep root and the fruit was ripe, questions were being asked that called for an immediate answer, and urgent desires had been stirred. If they had only looked they would have discovered around them *the fields* are *already white for harvest*. There was some reproach in his tone. Around them, there had been men and women with an awakened hunger for a word about the grace of God here and now, for the promise of the forgiveness that could transform their whole destiny without a moment's delay, an assuring word could have brought them into the Kingdom of God, but his disciples had failed to speak it!

No doubt as he spoke to them in this way, Jesus had the hope in his mind that by coming to know and listen to the woman, and by the close fellowship they would find with himself in the work ahead, he would be able to kindle in their own hearts something of his own pastoral concern for the human situation, his "passion for souls", and that they would begin to know what it meant to rejoice before God "as with joy at the harvest" (Isa 9:3).

A Word in Season

It is the fashion today within the Church to concentrate the energy of our ministry especially on those aspects of it which involve its direct influence on community life and lead it towards politics. We are at pains to avoid the accusation that we are concerned only with the response of the individual to the Gospel, and with the saving of souls. The results of "evangelism" seem to come too quickly and easily to be genuine. The preaching "crusade" is suspected of being too one-sidedly triumphalist in its approach and expectations. Moreover there is the feeling often expressed that we have in our day entered a "post-Christian era" when we face around us nearly everywhere an alien culture unresponsive and immovable by the appeals that brought religious revival and renewal to Churches in past generations.

Certainly today we must not underestimate the need for the quiet and steady work that so naturally absorbed the disciples of Jesus. There is much in his teaching that is meant simply to be disseminated, and as it is gradually absorbed by the human mind it will become powerful in its effects. It will act like leaven in the dough gradually penetrating and influencing personality and society too, even at times fermenting revolution.

Therefore we must not underestimate the need to sow and wait, and perhaps to suffer as we wait. The example of Jesus' own life encourages us to zeal in such a ministry, for it was only after he gave himself up patiently to his death, that the glorious harvest of Easter and Pentecost began to take place. "Unless a grain of wheat falls into the earth and dies, it remains alone; but if it dies, it bears much fruit" (John 12:24). We have to learn to our own cost that "*one sows and the other reaps*". We are given many words in the New Testament about our need for patience. "Let us not grow weary in well-doing, for in due season we shall reap, if we do not lose heart" (Gal 6:9).

Yet the Gospel Jesus left us to proclaim still lends itself equally to reaping as well as sowing. He described the Kingdom not simply as being like a seed to be sown, or like leaven to be inserted in the meal, but also as being like a great supper with "all . . . now ready" (Luke 14:17) where the host ordered his messengers to "compel" the hungry, and the poor, and the desperate to enter and feast freely here and now, to enjoy liberty, wealth and satisfaction.

As we read through the New Testament Epistles we find the Apostles bringing before us in their preaching two distinct and important aspects of what Christ came to do for us, and of what he offers us here and now in this life. They call on us to receive the gift of sanctification, thus yielding ourselves through the powerful influence of the Spirit, in Christ, to a growing process of change which will be completed only in the world to come.

Yet alongside this gift of sanctification there is the offer of a quite distinct gift of free justification. As we receive Christ we receive a new status before God, the whole past guilt of our sin is completely blotted out, and we receive joyful assurances about our eternal destiny. Too many of us, by our short-sightedness, deprive ourselves of the enjoyment of the whole wealth which Christ seeks to share with us. Moreover, in our service of him we become like the disciples whom Jesus had to reproach so keenly. We allow a one-sided zeal for only one main aspect of the task of the Gospel to absorb all our energies.

We too become victims of our own planned routine of ministry, making ourselves sensitive only to certain aspects of human life around us. We miss great opportunities and become in some measure insensitive to the deepest emotional and psychological needs, and to the most fundamental questions of the people we are meant to serve – needs and questions which call for a different emphasis and approach.

We need therefore today to lift up our eyes and *"look on the fields"*. This incident before us teaches us that it is not always obvious where and when we might find ourselves challenged to seek and pray for a harvest. How unlikely it seemed that this woman that morning was so prepared for his word. How unlikely it was that Zacchaeus who had hidden himself in a tree as Jesus passed was so ready to respond to the least encouragement. In the autobiography of J. B. Gough who was at one time a well-known American actor, he tells of the misery of his youth when every day he became hopelessly drunk. People despised him, and yet took no heed. "It seems to be now", he wrote, "that if one word of kindness had been spoken to me then – one touch of a loving hand – one look of sympathy from any human being had been given to me – I could have been led anywhere. But no man cared for my soul."

Jesus' reminder, *"others have laboured, and you have entered into their labour"* is still relevant to us today. Here and there today seed sown in past generations is still ready to bear fruit, and that fruit can be harvested. The influence of centuries of Christian tradition has by no means been eradicated from the thought patterns and the basic desires of many people around us. The shape of the modern mind has not yet thoroughly hardened into such an alien mould that it cannot be even immediately impressed by the clear and simple presentation to it of Jesus Christ and the Christian faith in language using the same modes of expression as are used in the New Testament. Memories are there to be stirred, stored wisdom is ready to come to the surface, and young minds often find something that they can relate to in old poems and hymns and books. I had the experience of working with a young Christian in a Middle East country, strong and steadily growing in his faith. His conversion took place when he was studying seventeenth century English literature in the English class in an Arab university – John Bunyan and John Milton were responsible.

The Woman's Testimony and the Presence of Jesus

We are finally told of the remarkable happenings that took place in the village even before Jesus' visit, of the decisive part played by the woman, and of the word she spoke. Without any delay Jesus kept his promise that he would make her in herself a *"spring of water welling up into eternal life!"*. That we hear no more of the disciples may indicate that in such renewal movements, lay witness can be of first importance.

Though it was obviously quite spontaneous, her testimony can stand as a model even for today: *"Come, see a man who told me all that I ever did. Can this be the Christ?"*

She spoke of the new thoughts, hopes, and experiences that had come to her. She spoke of what she knew of him as *"a man"* – a person she knew to be completely human in his touch and understanding. When she spoke of her belief that he was *"the Christ"*, would she not have told how he led her to this discovery in that unforgettable talk that they had had together about worship and the seeking Father?

The evidence of the change of her life, her words about her experience, and her confession of faith created at first such an impression in her community that many people claimed to have believed simply because of her word. But the woman herself knew there had to be much more. She said "*Come and see*"! Jesus, we remember, said this to his two first disciples as they began to follow him (John 1:39). Philip said this when he was trying to win Nathanael (John 1:46). Our witness must lead people always towards personal encounter with himself.

She believed that he himself would not allow her effort to be in vain. He would be there waiting for them to come, as she tried to point and lead them to him. He himself would answer their prayers, as they pled with him to come amongst them. It was because of his own presence and his own word that they came to believe that "*this is indeed the Saviour of the World!*".

CHAPTER 12

THE HEALING OF THE NOBLEMAN'S SON

At this time in his ministry Jesus, according to John, had already done many miracles in Jerusalem. Moreover, according to the other Gospels he was healing many people miraculously in Galilee. John, having selected for us two examples of the kind of pastoral conversation into which he must have entered also with many around him, now selects for us two examples of the miracles of healing which he regarded as being fit to take their place among the series of signs he has selected in order to share with us his impression of the glory of Jesus. In the first of these, his account of the healing of the Nobleman's son at Capernaum, he illustrates for us how Jesus by coming near to us in this world draws out, inspires, trains, and rewards our human faith, and how through such inspiration to believe and pray he opens up before us great new possibilities for breaking out of our tragic human bondage.

John 4:43 – 54

43 After the two days he departed to Galilee. ⁴⁴For Jesus himself testified that a prophet has no honour in his own country. ⁴⁵So when he came to Galilee, the Galileans welcomed him, having seen all that he had done in Jerusalem at the feast, for they too had gone to the feast.

46 So he came again to Cana in Galilee, where he had made the water wine. And at Capernaum there was an official whose son was ill. ⁴⁷When he had heard that Jesus had come from Judea to Galilee, he went and begged him to come down and heal his son, for he was at the point of death. ⁴⁸Jesus therefore said to him, "Unless you see signs and wonders you will not believe." ⁴⁹The official said to him, "Sir, come down

before my child dies." ^{50}Jesus said to him, "Go; your son will live." The man believed the word that Jesus spoke to him and went on his way. ^{51}As he was going down, his servants met him and told him that his son was living. ^{52}So he asked them the hour when he began to mend, and they said to him, "Yesterday at the seventh hour the fever left him." ^{53}The father knew that was the hour when Jesus had said to him, "Your son will live"; and he himself believed, and all his household. ^{54}This was now the second sign that Jesus did when he had come from Judea to Galilee.

The Faith that Rebels

At Capernaum there was an official whose son was ill. Indeed, as far as the doctors were concerned, the child was *at the point of death*, and there was no hope. The neighbours were showing their sympathy, for many of them already knew by personal experience how hard it was to wait by such a death bed, and to watch the strength of a little one ebbing away so relentlessly day by day. Some of them had found comfort simply in resignation. Life was hard in those days and people learned to say "The Lord gave and the Lord has taken away" (Job 1:21). They were ready to help each other overcome sorrow with such fortitude in face of what they believed to be God's will.

Yet in this one home something had happened to a father which made him refuse to accept such an outlook or to take such a way. He knew the Word of God. It did not always teach such resignation. He knew promises made by God that inspired prayer and hope in such desperate situations. He knew stories of prophets to whom anxious parents in rebellious mood had turned in prayer for their dying children, and God had heard them. (1 Kings: 17:23, 2 Kings 4:18 – 37) He could remember words about a God who could interfere powerfully in life, who in feeding his flock would "gather the lambs in his arms" and "carry them in his bosom" (Isa 40:11) But above all he knew that Jesus was moving around the country teaching about God and his Kingdom. He was possibly not too far away. Perhaps this man had already seen and heard him. Might he not be the Messiah sent by God to save? Had he not at times laid his healing hands on the dying, and spoken words that brought blessing to little ones even at the point of death? Possessed and compelled by such words which he believed to be from God, he made his own decision. He could not possibly resign his child to death. He must seek first the fulfilment of all these promises. He must, above all, seek the help of Jesus.

Such was the background to the faith of this nobleman whose approach to Jesus finally brought about one of the remarkable signs recorded for us in this Gospel. Even though Jesus could also work equally powerfully without such faith being present, it it important for us to know how eagerly he searched for such faith among the people who came to him, and how inspired he was when he found evidence of it.

Pioneer and Example

We can regard the nobleman of Capernaum as a pioneer and example in a very important field of human life and thought. The arguments which the story compels us to attribute to him, found their echo in a popular religious book published in the 1920s. It reminded us that while many in Jesus' day accepted disease, paralysis, blindness, leprosy and death as part of life, Jesus himself did not do so. He rejected these and set out to banish and destroy them. His was a faith that rebelled where others resigned. The author pled with us to seek and cultivate such faith. Even though circumstances might force us to accept at times the inevitable sufferings and limitations that life brings to us we must accept them not with resignation to what we suppose to be the "will of God", but with a rebellious faith which resolutely and positively says, "This is not what God meant life to be when he planned it".

Such a rebellious faith, the author insisted, must inevitably affect our approach and attitude as we ourselves face life's most difficult challenges and problems. The claim was also made in this book (as in much of the Christian literature of the same period) that we owed the will to progress in medical science and the success which had so far been achieved in overcoming diseases, to this new and outstanding inspiration to faith given to us by the presence and example of Jesus in this world. Moreover, it was also held that progress in social and personal morals, and the attainment of humane and healthy standards in public entertainments and sports, were also due to the growing influence of the same Christian faith which impelled people continually to refuse to accept what was debasing and cruel, or to settle down at ease with what offends the Christian conscience.

Not long ago, after hearing of one more divorce among my friends and of another venture into living together outside marriage, I expressed in general terms to a younger colleague in the ministry my regret that even within church circles our moral standards in many aspects of personal life were slipping so badly. The reply was chiefly a shrug of the shoulder. I was told that today I must learn more readily to accept life as it is, and to live in and with the real world around me. My response was the simple argument that Christ lived, taught, died and rose again to prove that nothing contrary to his Word and teaching can ever now be accepted as if it were just a part of life. We must see such things as tragedy, indeed as the work of an enemy of life.

Does our Christian faith not know Jesus today just as this nobleman did – present in the world around us, telling us about a God with whom nothing is impossible (Matt. 17:20, 19:26) and inspiring us with such hope in face of even the desperate problems of our life, that we can never allow our minds to slip back into despair or fatalism or even into pessimism on any great issue?

Difficult Journey and Testing Encounter

Rumour had it that Jesus was at Cana, possibly a day's journey away. Yet the journey might have been longer, for he was prone to move on quickly from place to place.

We must not therefore underestimate the difficulties the man had to overcome and the apparent risks he had to take in making his journey to Jesus. Seldom, indeed, in any of the Gospels do we read of anyone being forced to put so much at stake in order to gain the attention of Jesus. Dare he leave his wife and family at such a time to face a long period of tense anxiety with the child helpless in such a critical state? His venture could be criticized as callous and foolhardy. Indeed the faith he was able to summon in order to make the journey was as marvellous as the very miracle he was going to seek from Jesus. Whatever circumstances arose, whatever the outcome of his desperate venture, he believed Jesus would not fail to honour the trust and hope that he had inspired.

On his arrival in Cana, there took place a tense and dramatic first encounter. Jesus himself was at this time beginning to face the acute problem which continually dogged his ministry. In his recent visit to Jerusalem he had acquired a great reputation for his signs and miracles. News had spread, and now even in Galilee he was finding himself acclaimed and sought after by many people as a modern wonder-worker, a sensation. They admired his success, and his technique, and of course they wanted him to keep on demonstrating. But their attitude was, in his view, perverse. The more familiar they became with the kind of work he was doing the more it was being proved that *a prophet has no honour in his own country!*. They were prepared in his presence to marvel, but never to worship, or to give him their whole personal trust. They were not listening seriously to what he said about the Kingdom of God. Nor were they seeking to enter it, and experience God's forgiving and transforming love. They preferred excitement to salvation. It was a sign of Jesus' humanity that he felt baffled, lonely, and troubled in heart as he found such people coming round him in droves. We are not surprised therefore that when this man finally reached him he experienced momentarily the backlash of these troubled feelings. Was this rather wealthy-looking man from Capernaum not just another of them – drawn not by his Word, his converting message, but only by his miracles; seeking not to enter into his Kingdom or friendship, but just to see some sign of his astonishing power?

The word which Jesus spoke to him: "*Unless you see signs and wonders you will not believe,*" was a question about his motive rather than an accusation. The man knew that Jesus was not trying to turn him away but was simply testing him.

In the man's impassioned and repeated cry: "*Sir, come down before my child dies*", Jesus heard more than a request for a physical miracle. He heard an affirmation of genuine personal faith, a cry of recognition, a commitment to complete surrender, a promise of trust whatever his decision, be it Yes! or No! "Lord I want *You*. I want your Kingdom and Glory as well as your power. I want your God as my God, your thoughts as my thoughts, your ways as my ways. I want my home to be yours too, my children to be your servants. Come down into our midst and tranform everything!"

His sincerity, his prayer, the tone of his voice in these few pleading words drew Jesus into immediate response.

"Sir, come down before my child dies "

Jesus spoke the word, *"your son will live!"* The boy, we finally know, was healed the moment Jesus spoke it. Nothing else was needed. Even when he was amongst us in the flesh, distance made no difference to his divine power to heal or bless where he willed. Exalted as he now is, he has the same compassion, and is no less powerful in the word he is able to speak.

This venture in prayer for a child in critical need takes its place alongside other stories recorded in the Gospels about the readiness of Jesus to hear the prayers of distracted parents and to restore family relationships that have been tragically broken, reminding us again that he is the Messiah who comes to turn the hearts of fathers to their children, and the hearts of children to their fathers (Mal. 4:6). Such stories are all meant to encourage those of us who have the same kind of family problems to take them to Christ today with persistent faith. They are not there to delude us with false hope.

Today, however, it should not be only our own felt personal and family need that drives us to Jesus on behalf of the child in our midst. When we think even of one, we cannot avoid allowing our mind to turn to the dangers that threaten all.

In the world environment and cultural climate in which we live, we will inevitably find ourselves re-echoing the prayer of the nobleman in its plural form: *"Sir come down, before our children die"*: As this sermon is being prepared for printing we have just received a fresh series of pictures of children in Ethiopia at the point of death. A week or two ago there were harrowing pictures accompanying newspaper articles about what it meant to be a child in one of the occupied areas of

Palestine and in Cambodia. Nearer home, too, the future of the child in our world is increasingly threatened by the carelessness with which we so often irrevocably pollute our atmosphere in pursuit of what we imagine to be prosperity, and by the slowness with which we make progress among the nations in nuclear disarmament. We can link up with the same prayer or concern over the increase in our society of child abuse, and of the homelessness and exploitation of juveniles, the spread of the kind of literature and entertainment which is calculated to trap the innocent, to deceive and pervert the mind, and destroy character. We can express through the same petition our concern over the increase through divorce of broken homes.

We have therefore to pray for the whole world today as we pray for our children. It is even more difficult to persevere in offering such prayer, than in naming one particular child and seeking a particular answer. The obstacles to the large scale progress we seek are so enormous, so political, so complicated. We seem to be asking for the reversal of years of social, industrial and moral habit. Here indeed we seem to be praying for the removal of mountains.

Yet the prayer as it is worded for us here is simple. It is a prayer for Christ to come into our world's life and control the decision of rulers and people where all these important issues are at stake. It echoes the prayer of Moses facing what for him were equally daunting difficulties. "If thy presence will not go with me, do not carry us up from here" (Exod 33:15). As we pray it we address one who has already proved his love for the world by sending his own Son to save us from perishing. Has he not put so much into it already that he cannot possibly forsake it? By coming once, has he not shown us that he can come again and again?

We must therefore persist. It was Jesus' own purpose to call us to this prayer when he taught us to say "Thy Kingdom come. Thy will be done on earth as it is in Heaven."

Jesus himself once or twice showed us that the obstacles before us in way of the progress of his Kingdom, would appear to us like a great mountain impossible to dislodge. He was reminding us of the prayer of the Old Testament Prophet to whom in his day the difficulties were no less formidable. But he knew how they could be overcome. "O that thou wouldst rend the heavens and come down, that the mountains might quake at thy presence!" (Isa. 64:1). "*Lord, Come down!*" "What is impossible with men," said Jesus, "is possible with God" (Luke 18:27).

The Word for the Way Ahead

The Word which Jesus spoke was brief, "*Go your son will live*". Yet he put into it everything he had to give to the man himself. It immediately brought him new life and hope. He had been given no proof, no sign, yet a miracle happened in his own mind. His anxiety was gone. *The man believed the word that Jesus spoke to him, and went his way.* Everything was changed, everything was done, because the Word had been spoken!

Hannah in the Temple at Shiloh one day had come to the end of her tether. For years she had carried a heavy burden of vexation and sorrow. It suddenly came to a climax in uncontrollable weeping and a desperate prayer. Then a word was given her by the priest which she felt able to take for certain as the Word of God. He had granted her petition. In due time she would have the child she had longed for. There was no proof, no other pledge than a mere word – from God. Yet it was as if everything had already happened. She "went her way, and ate, and her countenance was no longer sad" (1 Sam 1:13 – 18). A whole future assured in a mere word!

As it did to Hannah or to the man in our story so it can happen to ourselves. It can happen as we read the Scripture or hear it read. It can happen in other ways – for example through the word of a friend inspired to meet a need. A word comes to us – as if from God himself. It holds us, and we hold on to it. It can alter our mood and our outlook. It can sustain our hope and courage day after day. Elijah after the word of the angel, "went in strength of that food forty days and forty nights" (1 Kings 19:8).

Commentators on this incident have often likened this man's journey home to our own journey through life. He had to spend the night in Cana. Did doubts not begin to assail him? On the journey as he was beginning to be overcome by his disbelief others came to him and gave their news and their witness. How much it helps us to compare notes with others on the way and to hear it re-told us when it is slipping away from us by ourselves!

The apostle Paul having become depressed on his journey to Rome, when he met some Christians who had come to meet and talk with him, was able to "thank God and take courage" (Acts 28:15).

CHAPTER 13

AT THE "POOL OF BETHESDA"
John 5:1 – 18

5 After this there was a feast of the Jews, and Jesus went up to Jerusalem.

2 Now there is in Jerusalem by the sheep gate a pool, in Hebrew called Bethzatha, which has five porticoes. ³In these lay a multitude of invalids, blind, lame, paralyzed. ⁵One man was there, who had been ill for thirty-eight years. ⁶When Jesus saw him and knew that he had been lying there a long time, he said to him, "Do you want to be healed?" ⁷The sick man answered him, "Sir, I have no man to put me into the pool when the water is troubled, and while I am going another steps down before me." ⁸Jesus said to him, "Rise, take up your pallet, and walk." ⁹And at once the man was healed, and he took up his pallet and walked.

Now that day was the sabbath. ¹⁰So the Jews said to the man who was cured, "It is the sabbath, it is not lawful for you to carry your pallet." ¹¹But he answered them. "The man who healed me said to me, 'Take up your pallet, and walk.' " ¹²They asked him, "Who is the man who said to you, 'Take up your pallet, and walk'?" ¹³Now the man who had been healed did not know who it was, for Jesus had withdrawn, as there was a crowd in the place. ¹⁴Afterward, Jesus found him in the temple, and said to him, "See, you are well! Sin no more, that nothing worse befall you." ¹⁵The man went away and told the Jews that it was Jesus who had healed him. ¹⁶And this was why the Jews persecuted Jesus, because he did this on the sabbath. ¹⁷But Jesus answered them, "My Father is working still, and I am working." ¹⁸This

100

was why the Jews sought all the more to kill him, because he not only broke the sabbath but also called God his Father, making himself equal with God.

The Place

Jesus could not have personally approved of the strange goings on or of the superstitious ideas associated with the place.

The waters of the pool were now and then disturbed. People gathered and stayed round it because they believed that the first person who managed to immerse in the waters immediately after each disturbance would experience a cure from his disease. Since the disturbances were irregular, always one had to be on the alert, and great excitement was momentarily generated as the scramble into the water took place. Possibly several times a day they happened. They were numerous enough to keep the place popular. Large crowds were there. Stories circulated through Jerusalem about remarkable cures. Nobody had ever checked up on their genuineness. Of course the legends attached to the place grew, and it acquired an established tradition. No doubt, with smart business people around, it had become commercialized by those who sold snacks and perhaps hired out mattresses or seats.

We can think, however, of reasons why Jesus might have been attracted to visit such a place. Certainly one of them was to be found in the varied make-up of the crowd – onlookers, helpers, patients. Nothing really human was alien to Jesus and he must have loved being there and watching now one, now another, finding them interesting to look at simply as individuals, or recognizable as families. It must have been a keen disappointment to him later in his ministry to find that the crowds he had loved to preach to, showed so much hostility.

He was all the more attracted to this crowd because so many of them were in such a wretched condition – *a multitude of invalids, blind, lame, paralyzed*. He once said "when you give a dinner or a banquet, do not invite your friends . . . or your rich neighbours . . . lest . . . you be repaid. But when you give a feast, invite the poor, the maimed, the lame, and the blind, and you will be blessed". (Luke 14:14) In the parable of the Great Supper, the climax came when the servants were sent out "to the streets and lanes of the city" to "bring in the poor and maimed and blind and lame" (Luke 14:22). Here was the company amongst which, before God, he wanted to be found.

It is possible, too, that he found the place, and this crowd, attractive because the prevailing atmosphere was one of expectancy. Certainly, as we shall see, there were exceptions here and there, but many were there, even as casual onlookers, because they expected to see signs that here in this place miracles could happen. In spite of all the strange superstition attached to their hope they at least clung to the belief, so clearly encouraged by the Word of God, that ordinary men and women in trouble and distress need not resign themselves to sheer hopelessness, that people on earth can experience angelic visitation, that life in this world is open to another world, that the sick can at times by the mercy of God experience "divine" healing.

It is noticeable today that in the midst of Christian communities, alongside our Temples of orthodoxy there can appear quite often a "Pool of Bethesda". Those of us who belong to "mainstream" Christian denominations are being more and more forced to take notice of what we are tempted to call "fringe" religious sects which give support and fellowship to people who find us too rigid in our adherence to our traditional liturgy and practice, and lacking in enthusiasm. Sometimes in their own enthusiasm we find them verging on what seems to us superstition.

We have to be careful in our criticism, remembering that Jesus was not ashamed to pay his visit to Bethesda of old. I have often felt how helpful it would be if we shared something of their expectancy – especially at that point in the service when the Scriptures have been read and the sermon begins. How good it would be if we too at such a time even in the midst of our orderly routine would realise our close kinship with those at the Pool who, excited, lay there *waiting for the moving of the waters*. If only at times we ourselves could realise that what interrupts the ritual is better than the ritual itself! (cp. 1 Sam 3).

The Man

When Jesus arrived at the Pool on this particular occasion he found himself attracted by pure divine compassion to one lonely soul who in the midst of all the expectant hubbub had actually lost every vestige of faith and hope. He went straight to him and put a question which exposed the whole extent of his plight, *"do you want to be healed?"* The only answer he could give to Jesus' challenge was merely a pitiful and evasive complaint: *"Sir, I have no man to put me into the pool when the water is troubled, and when I am going another steps down before me."*

There must have been a time when such a straight question from Jesus would have received the immediately straightforward and positive response, "I do." But that was almost thirty-eight years ago. That whole length of time had passed with nothing ever happening to himself – always to others. All personal hope in his own case had gone with the years, and deep in his mind he had settled with himself that he would never make it. Habit had taken over.

The Pool had become to him personally what the Temple next door had become to many of its zealous attenders, or what a Church today can become to some of its "pillars" – a place of uneventful and unbroken ritual. The place itself had imposed its routine and taken over his life. He was there that day because he was there every day, and every day was the same. What kept him going in this way of life was the staying power of thoughtless habit.

The answer of this man to Jesus reveals another aspect of the sad plight which must have attracted Jesus to this man. In his moment of need he finds himself in complete isolation from all others. He confesses himself as lonely as he knows himself helpless. *"Sir, I have no man.* At the moment I most need help I find no one to turn to." We thus discover that even amongst the *"invalids, blind, lame, paralysed"*, so pitied by Jesus, when there was something to be gained, the competitive instinct took over, and at the crucial moment everyone proved to be out for himself.

We marvel therefore at what the coming of Jesus meant to this lonely heart. To the man who says "I have nobody", Jesus in effect says "I myself am here now at your side". The poor invalid did not know that it was Jesus, the Christ, the Son of God, who spoke these words, but he had now found the friend who had already by his sympathetic question begun to help him to overcome his troubles. Can we not read this as a sign of the care that Jesus desires to give, and to be given, to those who are beginning to lose hope in the course of our present ruthless competitive society?

The Word of Healing

Since his question, and its answer, had clearly demonstrated the man's hopeless lack of faith and will-power, Jesus could now therefore use the occasion not only to exercise his compassion in healing the man, but also deliberately to stage a remarkable demonstration of his otherwise hidden divine power and majesty (see p.106). The whole account of this incident and its aftermath makes it clear that he is here giving a unique sign, to any who will receive it, of who he is. He made the miracle happen as he made creation happen in the beginning – by a Word of omnipotent creative power. Those who witnessed it were reminded of the description in the 33rd Psalm of how God made heaven and earth: "For he spoke, and it came to be; he commanded, and it stood forth" (v.9). *Jesus said to him, "Rise, take up your pallet and walk" and at once the man was healed, and he took up his pallet and walked.*

Immediately after we read of how the miracle took place we begin to discover how closely people have been watching Jesus. We are told that *that day was the sabbath.* The command to the man to take up his pallet and walk was therefore a deliberate command to break the accepted rules of sabbath behaviour. Jesus' intention was deliberately to provoke the Jews into a confrontation for which he already in his mind had a well-thought-out answer. They fell into his trap. They challenged the man. They obtained his description of who had healed him, and they came and accused Jesus of his wrong-doing.

The reply Jesus gave was uttered not in defence or defiance but in the sheer majesty that had characterised every aspect of the miracle. *"My Father is working still and I am working."* They immediately understood what he was saying. It followed from their own teaching. Their theory was that God himself could be exempted from his own sabbath law. Indeed God was forced to work on the sabbath because he was God. He had to put out whatever effort was required to keep the universe going. The sun had to shine and the rain had to come even on the sabbath. Jesus here claims that he himself enjoys the same exception to the human rule as his Father himself. The Jews could not fail to realise now the equality with God not only in power but in privilege that he was claiming as they stood before him. He had driven his point home, and they had no excuse for ignorance as they determined more firmly than before that they must put him to death.

Pastoral Appeal and Pastoral Threat

The miracle which was to bring Jesus closer to his death also involved the healed man in trouble with the Jewish authorities. Jesus of course, was concerned for him and followed him up closely as he went to the Temple. We are not told everything that was said when he found him and spoke to him.

We interpret the report we have here as simply a short summary of what was said as Jesus expressed his pastoral concern. The recorded words reveal what was in the mind of Jesus at that moment, and give us insight into the message he sometimes gave to those he healed.

"See, you are well!" Jesus said to him *"Sin no more, that nothing worse befall you."*

We must read this as an appeal rather than as a warning. It is in the first place the same kind of appeal for gratitude and goodness that we find echoed everywhere in the New Testament. Of course the appeal is positive. We must sin no more simply because he has made us whole. He has set us completely free from the bondage and degradation of our past life, and made us new creatures. We do not need to return to our slavery or yield again to the sin that has held us down. We have to consider ourselves now "dead to sin and alive to God", and in sheer love and gratitude we have to make this the glorious dominant fact of our daily lives. (cf. e.g. Rom. 6:1 – 14) The Apostles learned such teaching from Jesus himself.

Why did Jesus on this particular occasion to his pastoral appeal add also a pastoral threat – a clear and solemn warning: *Sin no more, that nothing worse befall you?*

It is possible that in the case of this man there was a unique need to hear such a word at such a time. Jesus knows the make-up of each individual. Not all of us who have lived with ourselves for long will be able to claim that we were never at any time helped by the encouragement to goodness given in the occasional warnings offered by Jesus himself about the "unquenchable fire" and the "worm that does not die" (Mark 9:43 ff.)

We have seen that as he spoke this word of warning Jesus was anticipating his coming death on the Cross. Because he had brought such healing to mankind, he was now facing the worst thing that can befall any member of the human race. Shrinking as he was even now from the unspeakable and uncomparable horror of it, can we not think of him, knowing the weakness of this poor man before him, as pleading with him all the more urgently to turn away completely from the paths that lead mankind into such devastation and bitterness?

If there was occasion for such an utterance in the ministry of Jesus there is still occasion for its being repeated to us today in case for our own sakes we need to re-hear it. We must not become careless in a world where our salvation cost the death of Jesus himself. We dare not trifle with the sin that sent him to the Cross.

Jesus as Prophet, Priest, and King

A brief note is in place here on one feature of Jesus' ministry which from now on is given some prominence in John's Gospel.

We have pointed out that Jesus here seems to have made this man's healing the occasion for demonstrating his divinity and authority. He used it to reinforce his claim to be who he was. Yet there has been no doubt in our minds throughout the exposition that the whole incident is an act of pure divine compassion.

I can remember speaking to a group of students on Jesus' miracle of the healing of the paralytic in the second chapter of

Mark. I suggested that while Jesus healed this man out of compassion nevertheless at the same time he demonstrated certain truths about himself and his ministry. "How disgusting!" remarked one woman student. She pointed out that if we ourselves when we did some kindness to others, were at the same time consciously trying to teach them through our supposed act of love, some edifying lesson about who and what we are, then everything we did would be vitiated. When I listened to her I remembered how our teachers in divinity school used to warn us never to regard Jesus' miracles as proofs of his divinity. The warning would be deserved, and the argument valid in the case of any one of us other than Jesus. But with Jesus, it does not hold. As Augustine pointed out, Jesus himself is the Word of God. Therefore every act of the Word must itself be a Word.

Jesus in everything he does is always Prophet, Priest, and King. As our Priest he is all compassion, showing us a pity and love that is always genuine and pure. As our King he acts with majestic and miraculous power. As Prophet he inevitably teaches as he sets his love and power in motion. Everything he does in his work, is inevitably significant of who he is and of the redeeming purpose that has brought him into the world. We must rid ourselves of the idea that he could self-consciously switch about, playing different roles one apart from the other.

CHAPTER 14

THE WORKS OF JESUS AND THE BLINDNESS OF THE JEWS

Jesus Provokes Controversy

Having drawn the attention of his enemies away from the healed man to himself, Jesus spoke in his own defence, and delivered a discourse full of stinging accusations and warnings. This is the first of a series of lengthy utterances through which he provoked his enemies, and finally roused them into open controversy with himself not only in the Temple and streets of Jerusalem, but also even in Galilee. These public discourses are an important part of John's Gospel.

Whatever his circumstances Jesus had so much to say and give that he never spared himself. Even in his self-defence there was always a new self-revelation. At this stage in his ministry many in the crowd around him were still uncommitted, and his disciples also were there listening. Therefore the appeals and claims which he made even in addressing his enemies are as significant, eloquent and convincing as any he ever uttered.

It is not our purpose in this exposition of the Gospel to make any detailed analysis of the sentence structure, or of the meaning of the words used by Jesus. Nor within our available space can we draw the reader's attention closely to everything said. Our concern is to provide guidelines through the text so that the reader can have an understanding of the general drift of Jesus' thought, some illumination of the most important and outstanding sayings in their primary setting, and thus comprehend better his witness to himself.

The Reflection of the Father in the Work of the Son

John 5:19 – 20(a)

19 Jesus said to them, "Truly, truly, I say to you, the Son can do nothing of his own accord, but only what he sees the Father doing; for whatever he does, that the Son does likewise. [20]For the Father loves the Son, and shows him all that he himself is doing;

One of Jesus' most memorable sayings was to Philip: "He who has seen me, has seen the Father" (John 14:9). When we first reflect on these words we tend of course to make them refer to the moral and spiritual qualities which Jesus showed as a human being – his love, his patience, his righteous anger, his wisdom, his complete trustworthiness as a person, his trust in the Father as he underwent his passion. Here in our present passage, however, Jesus urges us also to see a likeness to the Father's work displayed in his own miraculous work. In that work he always knew himself to be closely under the Father's direct inspiration and guidance. He likens himself here to a son apprenticed to a father in a trade. The father demonstrates and the son copies.

Jesus was discouraged when people followed him because they saw his "signs and wonders", took up a superstitious attitude to his miracles, and neglected the more important aspects of his message. Yet here in this discourse he affirms decisively that if people would show reverence rather than superstition, then "these very works which I am doing" would "bear witness that the Father has sent me" (5:36).

The Son of God and Human Destiny

John 5:20b – 29

and greater works than these will he show him, that you may marvel. [21]For as the Father raises the dead and gives them life, so also the Son gives life to whom he will. [22]The Father judges no one, but has given all judgement to the Son, [23]that all may honour the Son, even as they honour the Father. He who does not honour the Son does not honour the Father who sent him. ²⁴Truly, truly, I say to you, he who hears my word and believes him who sent me, has eternal life; he does not come into judgement, but has passed from death to life.

25 Truly, truly, I say to you, the hour is coming, and now is, when the dead will hear the voice of the Son of God, and those who hear will live. ²⁶For as the Father has life in himself, so he has granted the Son also to have life in himself, ²⁷and has given him authority to execute judgement, because he is the Son of man. ²⁸Do not marvel at this; for the hour is coming when all who are in the tombs will hear his voice ²⁹and come forth, those who have done good, to the resurrection of life, and those who have done evil, to the resurrection of judgement.

His enemies, Jesus said, may have rejected the evidence of God's hand in the miracles they have already witnessed, but they are going ultimately to be forced to marvel as they become involved with the Son of God in *"greater works than these"*.

As this age comes to a close, two great final events will determine the future and place of each individual in the world to come – the raising of the dead, and the last judgement. Jesus here claims that he himself has been given the power and responsibility to do these *"greater works"*. This section of the discourse, therefore, comes to its climax in a description of how, in the words of the Creed, "he will come again to judge the quick and the dead" at the last day (vv. 28 – 9).

Before Jesus finally describes what will take place at this second coming, he reminds us that none of us need wait before we ourselves are in a position to know our own personal destiny when the last day comes. He speaks of how any one of us, if we will, can even here and now experience already eternal life and resurrection from the dead as we hear his voice today.

> *"Truly, truly, I say to you, he who hears my word and believes him who sent me, has eternal life; he does not come into judgement, but is passed from death to life. Truly, truly I say to you, the hour is coming and now is, when the dead will hear the voice of the Son of God, and those who hear will live."*

In this remarkable declaration he speaks clearly of the greatest and most miraculous work which God has given him to accomplish as long as this world lasts. The Father has put it into the power of Jesus to bring about for all of us who will hear his Word, and enter a believing relationship with him, a resurrection which *now is*. It transforms the life we are at present living on earth. It is the experience of a great inward liberation. It is indeed re-birth. It has happened. We know that we were dead, and now we already have eternal life. We were in darkness and now we see. We were in bondage and now we are free. We were guilty and now we are forgiven. It happened when we heard the Word of Jesus and put our trust in him. Such an inward resurrection also brings with it a great assurance about what will happen to us when we are brought face to face with Jesus the Judge at the last day, for it is the first instalment of what there and then will also take place, a preliminary foretaste of what will then be finally given. Indeed when it happens now, we know that the hour that is to come is indeed already here.

Jesus completes his description of these "*great works*" in a brief and dramatic picture of the final resurrection and judgement: "*The hour is coming when all who are in the tombs will hear his voice and come forth, those who have done good, to the resurrection of life, and those who have done evil, to the resurrection of judgement.*" He later added more detail to his description of this event in the parable in which he pictured all nations gathered before his throne, the separation of the sheep and the goats, and the judgement then pronounced on those who saw him hungry, thirsty, impoverished or imprisoned and who neglected their duty to him, and of the blessing pronounced on those who responded with compassion (Matt. 25:31 – 46).

Belief in these vivid New Testament descriptions is a vital part of the faith we confess when we repeat the Apostles' Creed. Though of course, it is impossible for us to conceive or imagine how these descriptions can be literal fact, nevertheless we are meant to hold before our minds the events they point to and allow our thought of them as happening, and our expectation of them as events, to motivate us to shape and to transform the way we live.

We are not meant to become perplexed or despairing. We

are reminded that it is those *"who have done good"* who are resurrected to eternal life, and those *"who have done evil"* who are damned. These words are meant to encourage us to live in love, fear and trembling as we wait in confidence and gratitude for Christ's coming. The one who gives us such confidence in waiting and serving is the one who comes in the end to put all things right.

The Inner Darkness of the "Jews"

John 5:30 – 40

30 I can do nothing on my own authority; as I hear, I judge; and my judgement is just, because I seek not my own will but the will of him who sent me. [31]If I bear witness to myself, my testimony is not true; [32]there is another who bears witness to me, and I know that the testimony which he bears to me is true. [33]You sent to John, and he has borne witness to the truth. [34]Not that the testimony which I receive is from man; but I say this that you may be saved. [35]He was a burning and shining lamp, and you were willing to rejoice for a while in his light. [36]But the testimony which I have is greater than that of John; for the works which the Father has granted me to accomplish, these very works which I am doing, bear me witness that the Father has sent me. [37]And the Father who sent me has himself borne witness to me. His voice you have never heard, his form you have never seen; [38]and you do not have his word abiding in you, for you do not believe him whom he has sent. [39]You search the scriptures, because you think that in them you have eternal life; and it is they that bear witness to me; [40]yet you refuse to come to me that you may have life.

Jesus now charges his hearers with the guilt of remaining blind and deaf in the midst of clear evidence of the truth they had decided to crush. They had stubbornly and deliberately closed their minds to the powerful revelation of God he had brought into their midst. They had complained that the witness he gave could not be truth because it was not corroborated by another person. In reply Jesus made a list of the supporting witnesses they were choosing to ignore. He mentions the Baptist whom in the early days of his ministry they had regarded as a shining light (vv.33 – 35). He mentions, again, his own works which were a convincing proof to those who care to heed them (v.36). He also mentioned the Scriptures "*It is they that bear witness to me*" (v.39).

The most damning accusation of all was spoken in these striking words: "*The Father who sent me has himself borne witness to me. His voice you have never heard, his form you have never seen.*" They are an expression both of reproach and encouragement. Jesus here sums up his entire Gospel in a few words. He had come so that if any around him were willing to listen they could at last hear the voice of God; so that if they were willing to look at the life he was living in their midst, they could see the form of God. And yet they had rejected it all. He also refers here to an inner witness which Jesus believed to have been given by the Father in the minds and hearts of those present around him as he went about his ministry – a witness which theologians have sometimes called "the inner testimony of the Holy Spirit". This, too, they were rejecting.

The Corruption of Social Values

John 5:41 – 47

[41]I do not receive glory from men. [42]But I know that you have not the love of God within you. [43]I have come in my Father's name, and you do not receive me; if another comes in his own name, him you will receive. [44]How can you believe, who receive glory from one another and do not seek the glory that comes from the only God? [45]Do not think that I shall accuse you to the Father; it is Moses who accuses you, on whom you set your hope.[46]If you believed Moses, you would believe me, for he wrote of me. [47]But if you do not believe his writings, how will you believe my words?"

In the Sermon on the Mount, Jesus pointed out that what determines whether our mind is full of either light or darkness depends on the orientation of the desire of the heart. The inner blindness which affected the "Jews" of his day was therefore due to the fact that contrary to their profession their inner motives and aims were debased and impure. "The eye is the lamp of the body. So, if your eye is sound, your whole body will be full of light; but if your eye is not sound, your whole body will be full of darkness. If then the light in you is darkness, how great is the darkness." (Matt. 6:23). Here in this passage Jesus develops the same theme, and applies it to his hearers. He warns them that we can see and receive the true light of God only if our hearts are oriented entirely towards God, and we are seeking the honour and praise of God alone. This is when our eye is "sound" (or according to the AV "single"). He probes the inner darkness of their minds, the darkness which has led them to reject him: "*How can you believe,*" he says, "*who receive glory from one another and do not seek the glory that comes from the only God?*"

In accusing them he draws a contrast between himself and them. He pointed out that in his own life he himself never for one moment sought any kind of honour from the world around him. Had he done so he could never have served God with complete singleness of purpose, or spoken the truth which the world requires to hear if it is to be brought to repentance. As for Jesus, here was the central rule of his life: '*I do not look to men for honour*' (NEB v.41). Here also was the point where the deepest difference between himself and all other men most clearly reveals itself: '*How can you have faith so long as you receive honour one from another, and care nothing for the honour that comes from him who alone is God*' (NEB v.44).

Here is the most devastating effect of the darkness in which they had allowed their minds to become engulfed. It had destroyed their sense of values and they had thus lost the power to discern clearly between what was genuine and what was false, what was worthy and what was unworthy. "*I have come in my Father's name, and you do not receive me; if another comes in his own name, him you will receive.*" Their inner blindness had given rise to a corrupting and deceptive social system in which honour was continually bestowed where none was due. Jesus had seen through it from the time he was a growing child. "Woe to you Pharisees! for you love the best seat in the synagogues and salutations in the market places" (Luke 11:43). Pride of place and love of earthly glory had bred self-centred personal ambition, competition for rank, and lust for precedence. Hypocrisy had flourished. "Woe to you who outwardly appear righteous, but inwardly are full of hypocrisy and iniquity" (Matt. 23:28). They were thus caught up in a vicious circle. So corrupting was the system that it inevitably prevented the recovery of a true sense of God.

The words of Jesus in this passage have to be interpreted strictly within the circumstances in which they were spoken. They refer to the particular set-up before him then. It need not always happen that the praise of men is corrupting. It is obvious that within a healthy society there must be some place for bestowing honour on people. We are urged in the New Testament to give honour to whom honour is due, and to recognize and thank God for goodness and worth where these show themselves. Jesus himself could remind his contemporaries that "the scribes and Pharisees sit on Moses' seat", therefore they were to be listened to with deference (Matt. 23:2).

Yet in our humanistic, elitist, market-oriented society, there is truth in the accusation that, leaving God out, we have again set up a value-system that in his sight encourages us to seek vain-glory one from another, and to give glory to what is worthless. Human pride and selfish ambition are nourished, and the achievement of personal glory is held out as one of our chief ends in life. In more recent years the attainment of excellence in athletics and sport has tended to become debased by its being linked up with vast financial rewards, and media fame. A radio commentator, on the subject of recent popular film, made the remark that "we have turned our villains into heroes".

I can remember Archbishop Temple, in an address to students, describing what had gone wrong with all of us. He said that our minds had become like a shop window into which overnight someone had broken. He had re-ordered the price tags so that what was of true worth was now marked cheaply, and the things that were of no value had the expensive labels attached. For us to get things right again meant undergoing a complete revaluation in our standards of value. We need to be continually recalled to a true sense of what is worthy of honour. In recalling us to the truth in this matter, Jesus offers himself as the example whose personal life demonstrates where glory should be sought and where it should be given. All the aims, values and ambitions of the world which crucified him are called in question by his consistent facing of the Cross. His resurrection declares that God bestows honour on those who honour him as he was honoured by Jesus. No society can ever be healthy where its standards of value are not basically determined by what shines out as worthwhile in Jesus. The first task of the Church is to help the world to see this, through seeing him.

CHAPTER 15

THE FEEDING OF THE FIVE THOUSAND
John 6:1 – 15   6:22 – 27

6 After this Jesus went to the other side of the Sea of Galilee, which is the Sea of Tiberias. ²And a multitude followed him, because they saw the signs which he did on those who were diseased. ³Jesus went up into the hills, and there sat down with his disciples. ⁴Now the Passover, the feast of the Jews, was at hand. ⁵Lifting up his eyes, then, and seeing that a multitude was coming to him, Jesus said to Philip, "How are we to buy bread, so that these people may eat?" ⁶This he said to test him, for he himself knew what he would do. ⁷Philip answered him, "Two hundred denarii would not buy enough bread for each of them to get a little." ⁸One of his disciples, Andrew, Simon Peter's brother, said to him, ⁹"There is a lad here who has five barley loaves and two fish; but what are they among so many?" ¹⁰Jesus said, "Make the people sit down." Now there was much grass in the place; so the men sat down, in number about five thousand. ¹¹Jesus then took the loaves, and when he had given thanks, he distributed them to those who were seated; so also the fish, as much as they wanted. ¹²And when they had eaten their fill, he told his disciples, "Gather up the fragments left over, that nothing may be lost." ¹³So they gathered them up and filled twelve baskets with fragments from the five barley loaves, left by those who had eaten. ¹⁴When the people saw the sign which he had done, they said, "This is indeed the prophet who is to come into the world!"

15 Perceiving then that they were about to come and take him by force to make him king, Jesus withdrew again to the hills by himself.

22 On the next day the people who remained on the other side of the sea saw that there had been only one boat there, and that Jesus had not entered the boat with his disciples, but that his disciples had gone away alone. [23]However, boats from Tiberias came near the place where they ate the bread after the Lord had given thanks. [24]So when the people saw that Jesus was not there, nor his disciples, they themselves got into the boats and went to Capernaum, seeking Jesus.

25 When they found him on the other side of the sea, they said to him, "Rabbi, when did you come here?" [26]Jesus answered them, "Truly, truly, I say to you, you seek me, not because you saw signs, but because you ate your fill of the loaves. [27]Do not labour for the food which perishes, but for the food which endures to eternal life, which the Son of man will give to you; for on him has God the Father set his seal."

A Planned Crisis in Galilee

Jesus was now in Galilee where he was still immensely popular. Many of his hearers believed that no prophet before him had ever spoken in such a challenging and liberating way. Yet many of them were attracted only by the more superficial aspects of his work and message, especially by his miracles. Obviously there was need for the issues to be clarified. Jesus hated being popular in the midst of pretence. He had made it as clear to those in Galilee, as he had already done in Jerusalem, where they were being led through his leadership and message, what he offered, and who he claimed to be.

His line of approach to the problem was carefully thought out. Everyone knew the story of Moses, regarded as the greatest of all the prophets. Moses himself had taught that the Messiah would be a prophet like himself (cf. Deut. 18:15). One of the greatest miracles of Moses had been to feed God's people with manna in the wilderness. Therefore many people believed that when the Messiah came he, too, would provide a marvellous feast for his people. They linked up this belief with the description of a feast which the Lord would provide for his people in a mountain place, at the time when he would clear up all the tragic mysteries of human life, "swallow up death for ever, and . . . wipe away tears from all faces" (cf. Isa. 25:6 – 8, Isa. 49:9 – 10).

Jesus therefore decided to gather the Galilean crowd round him in the kind of place which would fit in to the common expectations of the people. He would feed them. As well as giving them bread, however, he would there and then put across his chief message. As the Messiah, prophet and leader foreshadowed by Moses and foretold by the prophets, he had come not only to relieve the pressing earthly troubles of the people of God, but also to rid all creation of sin, death and our human darkness. He hoped in this way to force people to face up to the issues before them, and to decide whether or not they understood and believed his claims and promises.

The Miracle

Knowing that the crowds would eventually gather, Jesus carefully chose the place that would give the best setting for his sign – up among the hills in what one of the Gospels calls a "desert place". It had enough room for all he expected. People had gathered quickly as the news spread that he was in the area. Some had followed him here and there as he went round the countryside, some had come even from Jerusalem, and others were from local hamlets.

Many of them were bound to be hungry even before they arrived. The other Gospel accounts emphasise more than does St. John that in revealing his Messiahship Jesus also inevitably acted with spontaneous compassion. We can imagine his feelings as he looked on the crowd before him – their intent faces looking at him, the obvious signs of prevailing poverty, the couples, the children, the tired, haggard, and lonely ones. Of course he wanted to assure them that their Father who fed the sparrows understood and cared very much about their earthly needs. He had to offer them food. Yet his very compassion made him all the more anxious to tell them that they could not live by bread alone. They were made for God himself, for a greater freedom and destiny than this world can offer. He wanted them to know that he had come to lead them out of every form of earthly bondage to their final inheritance in the presence of God himself. He wanted to assure them that even there and then in the fellowship he would offer them, they could begin to know the blessedness of the purity of heart that could see God, that those who had a hunger and thirst for true righteousness would find satisfaction.

How majestically it was all done! It was organised as carefully as it was planned. Not a moment's hesitation! Jesus *knew what he would do*. Yet his consultation of the disciples was not a sham. He was genuinely open to their help and suggestions. Perhaps he was seeking their prayers and faith to support him in such a miracle! He was willing to let them do their part. Philip completely failed to read his mind or seize his opportunity. How gracious he was to take up Andrew's groping suggestion that he might use some of the resources that were already to hand. Looking back on his conversation with them the disciples felt he was testing them, and that they failed to grasp what he was going to do.

Yet even though they were not able to enter fully into his mind they nevertheless cooperated loyally in the part he actually gave them. The way they did it embellished what was done. It matters always to Jesus today that he has servants who do his bidding even though they might not always be perfectly in tune with his intention and will. Here where grace is so bountiful and free there must be order, reverence and a careful stewardship of what is given. The Church always needs pastors and office-bearers who follow faithfully Paul's precept "Let everything be done decently and in order" (1 Cor. 14:40).

Failure and Withdrawal

Jesus had hoped that the people would listen to him, that through the sign they might see beyond the sign. His plan had been to lift their minds, at least for a decisive moment or two, to what he had come to do for them and give them. He had hoped to gain their confidence so that he could begin to speak about himself as the true bread of life, the Word of God.

But he had not reckoned on the speed and nature of their immediate reaction. They believed they knew their real problems better than any prophet of God could tell them. They were not interested in anything but the earthly and the immediate. They wanted not the "bread of life" but political bread there and then in their hands! They themselves knew before he told them what "blessedness" meant. Before he could speak they came to take him over, to make him their leader in all the revolutionary plans they had already dreamed up in their self-centred, man-centred minds.

We can understand the drift of their thought. Jesus had made it clear that he was one of whom Moses had spoken. "*This is indeed the prophet who is to come into the world!*" There was irony in the situation. The extraordinary nature of the miracle had roused their excitement and had actually contributed to Jesus' own failure.

Certainly they wanted a religious Messiah but the religion was to be incidental. He was to be the warrior judge and King who would defend them from their enemies, restore the land and lead them into earthly prosperity. The miracle he had done proved to them that he was their man – powerful, down to earth, sensitive to the needs of ordinary humanity. How efficient, and well organised everything had been, how calm his bearing, how convincing the way he could manipulate a crowd of people! How gracious, too, his encouragement of the kind little lad whose lunch he had taken not to disappoint him! They decided to *take him by force to make him king*. The situation, they felt, was urgent. John the Baptist in Herod's prison had just been executed to satisfy the whim of his adulterous consort. There were rumours that the powers-that-be in Jerusalem were determined to kill Jesus himself.

We can therefore understand Jesus' problem. His thoughts were not their thoughts. Neither were his ways their ways. He had come into the world to set the pattern of a different kind of leadership. He had to become the leader who was pictured by one of the great Prophets, the Servant of God, who won his authority over his generation by being willing to suffer rejection by his unflinching adherence to the whole truth, even though his rejection would lead him as lamb to the slaughter in order to win recognition.

Bishop Holloway has recently suggested that Jesus at this point was faced again with the temptation he had already rejected in his refusal to turn the stones of the desert into bread. It was the temptation to convert his mission "into an instrument for the cleansing and re-ordering of humanity's political structures". As a desirable end this was so close to the real desire of Jesus as to present him with something of an inner crisis.

He did not dare even to show a sign of sympathy with his would-be followers. There was danger is this situation. The least compromise and he would soon have been identified with the most vicious aspects of their sometimes wild talk. He had to act with wisdom. He had to avoid the least suspicion of inciting revolt. They were in no mood to be reasoned with. Only one way was possible and he took it. He withdrew to the hills by himself. He felt he must withdraw his disciples, too. We are told in one of the other Gospels that he sent his disciples into a boat to go before him, while he went to the mountain to pray (Mark 6:45, 46). It was on this journey (of which we have given a separate exposition) that he gave to them the unique and unforgettable vision of his majesty and power as he came to them on the waters of the sea at night.

Accusation, Warnings and Appeal

The extraordinary miracle had such an effect on the crowd that they did not allow him to shake them off. Guessing the direction in which he had gone they found him next morning in Capernaum. They wanted to discuss the situation. It is possible that they were beginning to have second thoughts. Perhaps they felt now that they should have allowed him a chance to speak his mind before they tried to proclaim him as their leader. Perhaps he had something helpful to say about the political goals they cherished so dearly. Perhaps even in his own distinctive view of life and God, they might find inspiration for their social and political struggle. Perhaps they hoped that if they accepted some of his terms there could be a compromise.

Jesus, at this fresh beginning must have suspected their continuing militancy. He was aware from the beginning that the discussion might end disappointingly. Yet he welcomed the opportunity to talk in order to make clear what he had meant by the sign he had given. His approach showed respect for their zeal and activism. After all, their night journey had cost them effort and sacrifice, and they seemed prepared to commit themselves one way or another.

He lost no time in useless words of introduction. He was blunt in his opening accusation. Their reaction to his miracle had clearly revealed the low level of their desires, and their tragic blindness to the whole new world he had come to open up to them: "*You seek me, not because you saw signs, but because you ate your fill of the loaves*" – They had refused to look and think in order to see what the sign meant! They had missed his message about the Kingdom of God and had gained only the temporary satisfaction of one good meal!

Since their thoughts were moving on such an earthly level, his opening argument was on a very earthly level. He was as blunt in his warnings as in his accusation: "*Do not labour for the food which perishes, but for the food which endures to eternal life.*" His words echo the wisdom which for generations had been taught them as a people in the Word of God. They echo the 127th Psalm: "Unless the Lord builds the house, those who build it labour in vain. Unless the Lord watches over the city, the watchman stays awake in vain."

They are a reminder that no matter how ardent the effort, how noble the sacrifice and the heroism, how immense the amount of labour, put into the building of the house or the defence of the city, the whole great endeavour can prove in the end to be utterly in vain unless it is indeed a house of God that is being built, or a city of God that is being defended. His words also echo the searching quesiton of the Prophet in Babylon to his contemporaries in exile who were evading God's call to return to Jerusalem to rebuild their own city because they were fatally attracted to the profit and comfort which they imagined to be offered them by settling down where they were in doomed Babylon: "Why do you spend your money for that which is not bread, and your labour for that which does not satisfy?" (Isa. 55:2). We can indeed spend all the resources and devote the energies of our whole life to win in the end only false, short-lived, and empty satisfaction!

As we read through the account of what happened, we can sense that, beginning on such familiar ground, Jesus did make a deep first impression on his hearers that day. They knew enough about human wisdom and about life itself to know that there was truth in these sayings. Therefore in this context he can begin to speak about the "*food which endures to eternal life*" and to make his claims to be able to give it to them.

We shall see, as we read on, that Jesus failed on this second day, as he had on the first – not because his words were ineffective or misdirected but because they made their decision in face of the clear truth and went their own way. Let us not listen to the words we have just now heard from him merely as belonging to the record of an appeal that once failed, but as a reminder of one of his constantly reiterated warnings: 'What will it profit a man, if he gains the whole world and forfeits his life? Or what shall a man give in return for his life?' (Matt. 16:26).

CHAPTER 16

A DAY OF DECISION IN CAPERNAUM

John 6:28 – 63

28 Then they said to him, "What must we do, to be doing the work of God?" [29]Jesus answered them, "This is the work of God, that you believe in him whom he has sent." [30]So they said to him, "Then what sign do you do, that we may see, and believe you? What work do you perform? [31]Our fathers ate the manna in the wilderness; as it is written, 'He gave them bread from heaven to eat.' " [32]Jesus then said to them, "Truly, truly, I say to you, it was not Moses who gave you the bread from heaven; my Father gives you the true bread from heaven. [33]For the bread of God is that which comes down from heaven, and gives life to the world." [34]They said to him, "Lord, give us this bread always".

35 Jesus said to them, "I am the bread of life; he who comes to me shall not hunger, and he who believes in me shall never thirst. [36]But I said to you that you have seen me and yet do not believe. [37]All that the Father gives me will come to me; and him who comes to me I will not cast out. [38]For I have come down from heaven, not to do my own will, but the will of him who sent me; [39]and this is the will of him who sent me, that I should lose nothing of all that he has given me, but raise it up at the last day. [40]For this is the will of my Father, that every one who sees the Son and believes in him should have eternal life; and I will raise him up at the last day."

41 The Jews then murmured at him, because he said, "I am the bread which came down from heaven." [42]They said, "Is not this Jesus, the son of Joseph, whose father and mother we know? How does he now say, 'I

125

have come down from heaven'?" [43]Jesus answered
them, "Do not murmur among yourselves. [44]No one
can come to me unless the Father who sent me draws
him; and I will raise him up at the last day. [45]It is written
in the prophets, 'And they shall all be taught by God.'
Every one who has heard and learned from the Father
comes to me. [46]Not that any one has seen the Father
except him who is from God; he has seen the Father.
[47]Truly, truly, I say to you, he who believes has eternal
life. [48]I am the bread of life. [49]Your fathers ate the
manna in the wilderness, and they died. [50]This is the
bread which comes down from heaven, that a man may
eat of it and not die. [51]I am the living bread which came
down from heaven; if any one eats of this bread, he will
live for ever; and the bread which I shall give for the life
of the world is my flesh."

52 The Jews then disputed among themselves,
saying, "How can this man give us his flesh to eat?"
[53]So Jesus said to them, "Truly, truly, I say to you,
unless you eat the flesh of the Son of man and drink his
blood, you have no life in you; [54]he who eats my flesh
and drinks my blood has eternal life, and I will raise him
up at the last day. [55]For my flesh is food indeed, and my
blood is drink indeed. [56]He who eats my flesh and drinks
my blood abides in me, and I in him. [57]As the living
Father sent me, and I live because of the Father, so he
who eats me will live because of me. [58]This is the bread
which came down from heaven, not such as the fathers
ate and died; he who eats this bread will live for ever."
[59]This he said in the synagogue, as he taught at
Capernaum.

60 Many of his disciples, when they heard it, said,
"This is a hard saying; who can listen to it?" [61]But
Jesus, knowing in himself that his disciples murmured at
it, said to them, "Do you take offense at this? [62]Then
what if you were to see the Son of man ascending where
he was before? [63]It is the spirit that gives life, the flesh is
of no avail; the words that I have spoken to you are spirit
and life."

"I am the bread of life"

There are in this Gospel seven sayings of Jesus which begin with the words *"I am"* (cf.also 8:12, 10:7 – 9, 10:11, 10:14, 11:25, 15:1 – 5). Commentators who believe the number seven to have some significance to the writer of the Gospel point out that he also selected seven of Jesus' miracles to use as illustrations of the revelation of the glory of Jesus. Of more importance than the enumeration of such sayings or signs, however, is the frequent use which now occurs of the phrase "I am" in referring to himself. The use of this phrase can be regarded as a deliberate echo on his own lips of the name by which the God of Israel chose to make himself known to the people of Israel when he sent Moses to be their deliverer. "God said to Moses, *'I AM WHO I AM'* ". And he said, "Say this to the people of Israel, *'I AM'* has sent me to you". (Exod. 3:14).

The saying *"I am the bread of life . . ."* has always been given a central place among the texts which have inspired the devotion and worship of the Church. It seems to be a word given to us especially for our liturgy when we celebrate the Lord's Supper. Spoken to us in this setting it helps us to realise that the Supper is not merely a memorial service for one who lived and died centuries ago, but an occasion for communion with the one who has also risen again for us. It assures us that Christ is here and now in the midst, so near and real that we can enter into life-giving fellowship with him. Spoken along with the giving of the bread and wine it is a pledge to us that receiving him by faith we will find ourselves strengthened, enabled to grow in grace and in vision, and to become more deeply rooted and grounded in the love we must have both for our fellow men and women and for himself.

Apart from the Lord's Supper, how much these words bring as we allow them to come home to us in the midst of a day-to-day life. They remind us that at the heart of our Christian faith, rather than a creed or an ethical code, there is a person who meets and speaks to us, whose friendship is always open to us, and who is able to give us comfort in our deepest inward needs. Moreover, as he offers us himself, he also offers us everything most worth having in life not only for time but for eternity.

We should hear, along with the repeated saying, the assuring words that almost immediately follow: *"All that the Father gives me will come to me; and him who comes to me I will not cast out."* That he himself could ever act in the brutal way those words "cast out" literally imply, is so impossible to conceive that we know for certain that we are safe as we yield to the least instinct to come to him. Moreover, the twice repeated promise which soon follows: *"I will raise him up at the last day"* underlines the affirmation that in our present communion with him here and now, we already have the foretaste of eternal life to come.

Jesus Provokes Offence

The very words which have brought so much illumination and strength to Christians from age to age, brought when they were first spoken deep offence to their hearers. Their utterance indeed provoked a decisive reaction in the attitude of the crowd to Jesus just at a time when he had seemed to be impressing them with his wisdom and recovering their confidence.

Jesus had appeared to have his hearers in his hands. They were eager to ask him questions and to receive his answers. They expressed to him their desire to *"work the works of God"*, and they did not object when he suggested that this first of all meant believing in himself as God's messenger. They even accepted his claim that it was he himself, coming from the Father, rather than Moses, who could give them the *"bread of God"* which came *"down from heaven."* "Lord" they said, "give us this bread always." It is obvious that they would have been prepared to accept an offer from him to *give* them the "bread of life" if he had been prepared to make that simple offer.

When any teacher in those days referred to himself as giving bread to his hearers to eat, he was referring to the satisfaction that the truth he presented could bring to the human mind. The Old Testament spoke of God as "feeding" his people, when he inspired the prophets to speak his Word to them. The revelation of God given through the word is thus regarded as heavenly bread in contrast to earthly food. Even we ourselves today speak of the preacher as there in the pulpit to "feed the flock". (cf. Acts 20:28).

A Day of Decision in Capernaum*   129

If Jesus, therefore, in Capernaum that day had contented himself by saying merely: "I have come to give you the bread of life", they might have accepted his saying, and respected his claim. He could have been understood to offer simply a revealed teaching which brought satisfaction to the longing heart and searching mind.

Jesus, however, did not merely claim to have come to *give* the bread of life, he said "I *am* the bread of life". It was as astonishing a claim and as challenging a decision to faith in himself as he had ever given this Galilean crowd. It was the affirmation that if anyone willed to pursue his invitation to discipleship he could find in his own personal presence and friendship the communion with God for which they were made. Moreover it was the assertion that those who found what he had to give would never think of turning away from him to any other source of light or life.

It was at this point that the shock came to many even of his own so-called disciples among the crowd. They were enraged that this man seemed to be putting himself at the centre of everything good in the universe! He seemed, to place himself at the gate of the Kingdom of Heaven, with power to decide who shall be received and whom he will reject. He spoke as if he had this gift of eternal life in his own hands to give or withhold. They murmured, and said *"Is not this Jesus, the son of Joseph, whose father and mother we know? How does he now say 'I have come down from heaven?' "*

There was not the slightest attempt on the part of Jesus to tone down the point which had raised antagonism, the very point where his teaching was most relevant, and where there was a need to press on with it. Therefore the very words he used became more and more provoking as he responded to the tension between himself and them. He said, *"The bread which I shall give for the life of the world is my flesh"* and solemnly added, *"Truly, truly, I say to you, unless you eat the flesh of the Son of man and drink his blood, you have no life in you,"* insisting that only such eating and drinking of his flesh and blood would assure them of eternal life and resurrection at the last day. He further affirmed that he himself having come *"down from heaven"* would ascend where *"he was before"* because he was the *"Son of man"*.

Of course a long controversy developed of which we here
have only the barest outline. As the day wore on, they moved
from the streets into the synagogue. At the end of the day they
expressed their bitterness and disillusionment and *many of his
disciples drew back and no longer went about with him.* The day's
happenings marked the beginning of Jesus' alienation from
the Galilean community. It is to be noted that those who were
most vociferous in raising objections to what he said are
referred to as "*Jews*". The use of this word does not imply that
these objectors came from Jerusalem. They may have been
genuinely members of the local communities. They are called
"*Jews*" simply because there and then they took up a hostile
attitude to Jesus.

The Search for an Explanation

It is possible for us to find historical and psychological reasons
why Jesus at this stage of his earthly career should have been
so deliberately blunt as he faced this crowd from which he had
possibly hoped to win some disciples. He hated the pretence of
a superficial popularity based on a misunderstanding of who
he was, and what his claims really were. He did not want it to
continue. He was certain that the time had come for the issues
to be clarified. He once remarked: "Blessed is he who takes no
offence at me" (Matt. 11:6). He knew that many around him
in that crowd were living with beliefs that had to be challenged
to the point of their being "offended", if they were ever to be
brought to faith in himself. Therefore he was prepared at this
important point in his career to use this testing and
provocative language.

We find, however, that a number of commentators on the
Gospel find it impossible to believe that Jesus could have
spoken in this way at Capernaum.

They affirm that the reported words of Jesus can be
understood only if they are taken to refer to the Lord's
Supper, and they raise doubts as to whether he would at this
time have made such a reference. They object especially to the
crude language used. They doubt whether Jesus himself
would have spoken of our "eating the flesh" and "drinking
the blood" of the Son of Man. Some writers have suggested

that these words contain later reflections by the Church on the Last Supper; others have suggested that they contain a view of the Sacrament developed in the Church under the influence of the surrounding pagan mystery religions. There has also been the suggestion that such words were actually spoken by Jesus himself at the first celebration of the Sacrament in the upper room, and since John decided to avoid useless repetition in his Gospel with another full account of the Last Supper, he inserted them here.

Our "Mystical Union with Christ"

It is possible, however, to regard Jesus' words as having no direct or exclusive reference to the sacrament. John Calvin, for example, whose judgement on the New Testament is always to be respected, agrees that "it would be inept and unseasonable" for Jesus to preach about the Lord's Supper before he had instituted it. Therefore he wrote of our being called to enter a "mystical union" with Christ. His argument can best be understood if we grasp the purpose Jesus had especially in mind when he spoke to this crowd at this particular time.

From the beginning of the Prologue, and throughout the whole Gospel of John it is stressed that Jesus' work is both light-bearing and life-giving. He came into the world not only to reveal God to us but also to bring us into living communion with the life of God, not only to displace our darkness of mind with what he reveals in his life and teaching, but also to replace the prevailing human corruption and death that mark all our existence on this earth, with the gift of eternal life. Throughout this present discourse Jesus was speaking almost exclusively about the latter life-giving aspect of his ministry among us. This is why he referred several times to himself as having become incarnate (i.e. as having *"come down from heaven"*) in order to give life to the world.

There were however two conditions which had to be fulfilled if perishing men and women were to be able to benefit from his coming, and receive the life he gives. In the first place he himself had to die. When he spoke of his *giving* his flesh *"for the life of the world"* (v. 51) he was referring to the fact that only through his Cross could the world receive new life from him.

In the second place he insists in this discourse not only that he himself should be sacrificed but also that each of us whom he calls to come and believe in him should, by doing so, enter a close, intimate, and indissoluble union with him. It is only through such a union that the renewing power of the eternal life which he has come to give us can become effective within each of us.

It is this life-giving union between himself and us that Jesus made the central theme of his Bread of Life discourse when he spoke that day at Capernaum. He insists that in it we are both intimately close to him, and yet personally quite distinct from him. He is trying to convey to our minds its close and life-giving nature when he calls himself "Bread" which he urges us to receive into ourselves by eating. Yet he is also trying to impress on us its spiritual and personal nature when he stresses that the relationship between us and himself is always one of faith in his own Person and Word, and when he insists that his words are not to be interpreted literally but are "*spirit and life*".

At the heart of the relationship between himself and us therefore, he wants there to be always trust, friendship, understanding and following. Yet at the same time he wants something even deeper. He does not want to influence us simply by remaining outside of us as in an earthly friendship. He wants inside of us. When he speaks about his "flesh" and "blood" we can understand that he is referring not necessarily to the Lord's Supper but simply to himself in the humanity he assumed to save us. His challenge to us to "*eat the flesh of the Son of Man and drink his blood*" is a challenge to cultivate this union he is seeking to have with us through his humanity, and thus to allow an open entrance into our lives for the renewing power of his Spirit. It involves our seeking with our whole mind and heart to absorb into our lives the whole Christ in the humanity in which he is presented to us in the word, in his birth, life, teaching, death and resurrection. Is he not here seeking to discourage us from cultivating simply a mere "spirituality" which does not centre on, or orient itself towards the person he was, and the work he did for us as a human being? Might he not be warning us against the dangers of yielding uncritically to the promptings of any inspiration, however spiritual, that do not arise out of the Word of God as it witnesses to himself made flesh?

CHAPTER 17

JESUS AND THE DISCIPLES – I
John 6:16 – 21

16 When evening came, his disciples went down to the sea, [17]got into a boat, and started across the sea to Capernaum. It was now dark, and Jesus had not yet come to them. [18]The sea rose because a strong wind was blowing. [19]When they had rowed about three or four miles, they saw Jesus walking on the sea and drawing near to the boat. They were frightened, [20]but he said to them, "It is I; do not be afraid." [21]Then they were glad to take him into the boat, and immediately the boat was at the land to which they were going.

A Night Remembered

In three of the Gospels we hear slightly different accounts of what happened that night. It is obvious that each one who went through the experience remembered it vividly with different details in the foreground of their memory. The Apostle John never forgot the stress, the emotions, the strange thoughts and fears that arose, the relief that finally and suddenly came, and the lessons they then learned about life with Jesus.

They found themselves plunged suddenly into it. It was one of those dark and threatening nights on which they would normally not have chosen to venture out in a boat, but Jesus had given them the order without consulting them. John describes vividly how one thing seemed to follow another as soon as they were away from the land – the darkness growing more and more deep, the harsh contrary wind, the strange feeling of depression, a slight uncanny fear, and the loss of morale among the whole group. The worst thing of all was the strange questioning about Jesus. The expectations that morning had been great. The miracle of the bread had been so wonderful – and in the end it had all seemed to come to nothing! He had suddenly retreated when everything had seemed to be going his way. Had they ever before seen him so perplexed? Why had he so abruptly dismissed them when they had so many questions to ask, and wanted assurance? Why had he chosen this way for them to go on such a night? John's description of the situation seems to have a mysterious symbolic touch about it. *It was now dark, and Jesus had not yet come to them.* They had such a keen sense of his absence as they longed for his presence! So haunted had their minds become, so great their depression, that when they saw him coming over the waters, and drawing near them, *they were frightened.*

It was when they heard his voice that they knew that it was he. The assurance that came with the word he spoke, so completely banished all their doubts and fears that there was no need at the time to ask their questions or tell him what they had felt. *"It is I; do not be afraid."* His words reminded them of the name of the Lord of the Exodus who had so marvellously manifested his control of the fire at the bush and of the waves of the sea, when he led his people out of Egypt. And then marvellously they found themselves *immediately at the land to which they were going.* They remembered one of the great Psalms which perfectly expressed their thanksgiving.

> He made the storm be still,
> and the waves of the sea were hushed.
> Then were they glad because they had quiet,
> and he brought them to their desired haven.
>   (Ps. 107: 29 – 30)

An Easter Experience before Easter!

Of course the disciples were used to Jesus taking them apart from the crowds after the business of the day sometimes to explain any difficult things he had been trying to teach, and to review with them what had been happening. They could ask him questions and he would teach them privately. He had always shown as much concern to train them as a group, as he had to preach to the crowds. Indeed, as time passed, the less he found he could rely on the crowds, the more he realized he must depend for the future of his work and his Church on these few. The Church of the future would have a solid foundation only if this core of disciples had an adequate store of wisdom, strong faith, unflinchable loyalty and deep conviction. It was they who were to be sent out into the world under the inspiration of the Spirit to continue his work.

He was concerned therefore during his ministry on earth to be with them as much as he could, to win their complete trust, to help them towards a clearer and deeper vision of who he was and of what the future held. He had on occasion taken them into special "retreat" so that he could concentrate on teaching them. The disciples never forgot how thrilled he was on one of these occasions to discover that their faith in him had at last become like a "rock" on which he could confidently build his Church (Matt. 16:17).

They were always full of gratitude that before he gave himself up to death he took them all apart into the upper room for these last unforgettable hours of fellowship, cleansing and communion.

That strange night's retreat in Galilee came eventually to occupy a prominent place in their memory of these special times with Jesus, but it was only some time after Jesus died and rose again that they understood its full significance and meaning. It was indeed only after they set out on their mission to convert the surrounding world that the message he then taught them came fully home to their minds. The spread of the early Church under their ministry (as we read of it in the book of Acts) was of course marvellous, and in the long run they won the pagan world around them over to Christ. But the full story of their conquest was not always one of continuous and spectacular growth everywhere. As they tried to serve him, to do his will and to go the way he wanted in different places and in different times under different circumstances they discovered that the experiences of that night on the lake seemed occasionally to repeat themselves. They felt themselves being put through the whole cycle of it all again – the uncertainty about direction, the depression, the nervous

perplexity, the temptation to lose morale and to be edgy with
one another, the irrational fears – and then he, the Risen
One, had come to them. They had recognized his presence by
his voice ("my sheep hear my voice" he had said), they had
received him into their midst, and they had managed to attain
almost immediately what they had, under their depression
and difficulties, thought impossible. Here, then, was their
clue to the revelation Jesus had given them of himself and his
power on that memorable night on the lake. It had been an
Easter experience before Easter, it had been a rehearsal of an
act that was going to be repeated within his Church again and
yet again as time moved on.

As they recalled these Galilean days with Jesus therefore,
this incident on the lake took a prominent place in the
preaching and teaching to others, especially to those who were
to follow them in the leadership of the Church. No doubt they
found the way that Christ was leading them at times truly
expressed in one of the great Psalms which they often
remembered:

> Thy way was through the sea,
> thy path through the great waters;
> Yet thy footsteps were unseen,
> Thou didst lead thy people like a flock.
>
> (Ps. 77:19 – 20)

Our Way in the Sea

If our memories are long enough, we will not find it strange to
read in our hymn books the verse beginning "Like a mighty
army moves the Church of God".

At the beginning of the century many of our large city
churches (and many more that have been pulled down since
then) were full to the back of the gallery Sunday after Sunday.
The word of the Church was seriously listened to in the
nation's councils. The influence of the Christian faith was
strongly felt in family and community life. Even in the
thirties, when I began my ministry, its influence was still
powerful. We still had many listening to the Word of God, and
crowds of children and young folk around our doors. It did not

occur to us then that this was not a "Christian" country. To be a pastor in a congregation was like being up there on the mountainside, with many around us, and Jesus in full command. We could think of ourselves as marvellously feeding the multitude under his direction, and in spite of our own deficiencies, at least there were few who questioned the authority of his teaching.

Is there not a clue to what is now happening to us, here in this story of the disciples on the lake? We now have to set our face against an "encircling gloom", and threatening contrary winds, in a world where life in general seems to be growing more harsh for everyone, and more pagan. Public opinion and the "Spirit of the Age" are no longer allies we can trust to be on our side. Alongside that of Jesus, many other names are being called upon to bring us inspiration and salvation. Many of our own ardent and sincere efforts at our own renewal and recovery have proved fruitless. There are uncertainties and questionings in too many of our own minds about our message, and even among those who adhere most faithfully to it there can come at times that strange sense of the absence of Jesus, which is reflected in John's revealing confession of his own momentary desolation of spirit: *It was now dark, and Jesus had not yet come to them.*

John Mark in his account of this incident, has added a detail absent from this gospel. He reminds us that having sent them out on this journey, Jesus himself went up to the hills to pray, and that from his place "he saw that they were distressed in rowing" (Mark 6:48). He was praying for them, and watching, with care and concern for every detail. They were those whose welfare the Father had entrusted to him. He could not dare risk even letting them out of his sight in the midst of any possible danger. He knew what they could bear, and he was ready to go to them if things ever became unbearable. He was praying that their faith might grow and that they would learn what it meant to trust and obey him when the way was hard and they did not understand.

So with us, even though we do not see him, he is there at the right hand of God making intercession for us. "Christ loved the Church and gave himself for it" (Eph. 5:25). How much he cares for us! He wants us to learn to walk by faith and not by sight; to endure when things are hard and there is no sign of success; to believe and go forward when there is no apparent way open before us; to obey where we do not understand, simply because we hear his voice. Like the disciples, everything depended on our recognizing him by his voice. Our doubts disappear when we hear him speak again to us in his own unmistakable words that assure us of his presence.

Then they were glad to take him into the boat, says the original story. Even if nothing else in our circumstances seems to change, what a difference it immediately makes when we are assured that he is present in our midst as our companion on the difficult journey. Mark in his account says that immediately their circumstances did change and "the storm ceased". But John does not mention this. As it happened, he hardly noticed it. The one thing he did remember was how soon they got through. It had all seemed so nearly impossible, but they were there: *Immediately the boat was at the land to which they were going.*

No doubt for some of us this way across the sea becomes a very personal story. The Good Shepherd does not treat us simply as units of a flock under his care, but plans or leads us each in the way we have to go as individuals, calling his own sheep by name. The way he chooses can sometimes be through the dark and threatening valley, under strain and stress. Life grows hard, our personal situation seems to be hemmed around with darkness, and our hold on it grows weaker. We too can learn from this very incident, not to let go in despair. He will come. We will hear his voice. Nothing around us will prevent his taking us to the very destination we have sought and he has planned.

Encounter in Apartness

This remarkable manifestation of the presence and power of Christ which was finally to prove itself so inspiring and memorable, presents to us one feature which we must not overlook. It was given to the disciples by Jesus after he had completely withdrawn them, as he had himself too, apart from the multitude amongst whom they had been busily at work. Indeed, he could not have conveyed to them either the sign or the message he felt they needed so much, had he not brought them to this secret rendezvous. It is significant that during the hours he spent with them, apart in the upper room, he made a promise that the intimacy he had established with them during such time of retreat would continue in the days ahead. He promised that he would come back specially to manifest himself to them and strengthen them through the Spirit, again and again, in apartness from the world. "I will not leave you desolate", he said, "yet a little while, and the world will see me no more, but you will see me" (John 14:18 – 19). This promise of encounter in apartness of course was fulfilled during his Easter appearances. During these memorable forty days it was always quite apart from the world that the disciples knew him present and were strengthened, taught and encouraged.

After his ascension they continued to find themselves es-pecially conscious of his presence with them as they gathered apart "devoting themselves to the apostles' teaching and fellowship, to the breaking of bread and the prayers" (Acts 2:42).

Of course he had sent them out with the great promise, "I am with you always" (Matt. 28:20). They knew well what it meant to find themselves by his present help victorious in the struggles they had to face as they obeyed his command to go into all the world and serve him. But his last great command and promise did not cancel out their continuing need to come apart so that he could come to meet them.

The exalted Christ by his ascension has taken himself apart from the world into which he has sent us to evangelise and to engage in his service. He has gone to his own realm, from which he is prepared to come to us again and again to enter intimate, enriching, and empowering dealings with us. Certainly he has not forsaken the present realm of this world and its history. It is under his providence. It is protected and preserved by his prayer. Its future is his deepest concern because he has died for its salvation and he is coming again to claim it for himself and to judge all. But it sees him no more, as we who are his own can do when we lift up our eyes, our faith, and our hearts to seek him in the world above, where he has gone. Even as we rely on his promise to come and be with us always we ourselves have to learn the discipline of turning aside from life, to allow him to meet us.

CHAPTER 18

JESUS AND THE DISCIPLES – II
John 6:64 – 71

[64]"But there are some of you that do not believe." For Jesus knew from the first who those were that did not believe, and who it was that should betray him. [65]And he said, "This is why I told you that no one can come to me unless it is granted him by the Father."

[66]After this many of his disciples drew back and no longer went about with him. [67]Jesus said to the twelve, "Will you also go away?" [68]Simon Peter answered him, "Lord, to whom shall we go? You have the words of eternal life; [69]and we have believed, and have come to know, that you are the Holy One of God." [70]Jesus answered them, "Did I not choose you, the twelve, and one of you is a devil?" [71]He spoke of Judas the son of Simon Iscariot, for he, one of the twelve, was to betray him.

Jesus, Triumphant and Tense

In a few verses in the middle of his discourse on the Bread of Life, Jesus had given some indication of his own thoughts as he reflected on both the successes and the difficulties he was having in his ministry. He affirmed his faith that everything that was taking place of any final significance, was what was decreed by the Father (v.37). He expressed his own confidence that he himself had in no way failed God's purpose (vv.38 – 39). He was certain that everything he had done would be vindicated in the last great day of judgement (v.40). Neither the power of evil, nor the human will, could in any way prevent the salvation of one of those whom God the Father had chosen (v.39).

At the end of the discourse the evangelist himself returns to this theme. Jesus, he assures us, knew from the beginning the failure he was going to have to face on that particular day, yet he was confident all the time that God's hand was there triumphantly at work. Then he gives us an account of how Jesus' serene confidence found its final expression in the challenge he uttered as he turned to the twelve and said *"will you also go away?"* This is not to be interpreted as an appeal to his disciples for their help in bringing in his Kingdom. It is an expression of personal triumph. It is the elated utterance of one who, while he moves on to assured victory, needs nobody, but who desires to share his kingdom with those he loves.

Amidst such expressions of supreme confidence, however, there is evidence that Jesus was often also perplexed. He saw clearly the grim and tragic consequences of the rejection of his good news by so many around him. We cannot help noticing the urgency and anxiety with which he made his appeal to them to respond to him, promising that he will not reject any (v.37). He expressed amazement at the perversity that kept people back when they could have easily decided otherwise. The comment *"There are some of you that do not believe"* was a reproach for their stubbornness. He felt the tension all the more deeply because he was trying so hard to win them, and his heart was open. Satanic powers, too, were at work here frustrating the will of his Father! *"One of you is a devil!"*, was his final comment as he looked at the twelve. Such powers had to be resisted even to death, and here they were, apparently triumphant, even amongst those he had chosen as his own, because he had not doubted their loyalty. He seemed to feel himself in the midst of an on-going conflict between God and the Devil.

In the end, of course, in one of his last recorded prayers to the Father, as he looks back and sums up what has happened it is the note of triumph that he sounds most clearly: "I kept them in thy name which thou hast given me. I have guarded them and none of them is lost but the son of perdition, that the scripture might be fulfilled." (John 17:12) God was certainly working his purpose out, even in the midst of what had caused him so much anxiety and trouble. Yet the tension, even to the end was real. Simon Peter was undoubtedly his own, and yet he kept hold of him only by intense prayer: "Simon, Simon, behold, Satan demanded to have you, that he might sift you like wheat, but I have prayed for you that your faith may not fail" (Luke 22:31).

We can recognize as we read the New Testament that the first followers of Jesus, after he rose again, shared the same triumphant certainty that he was Lord of all and that in the end all things would be put under his feet. They emphasised the sovereignty of God so much that they attributed every work of salvation to his grace and power alone. People were saved because he had predestined them to be saved. More-over, behind the deliberate obstinacy of those who rejected the Gospel they tended also to see the hand of God, hardening the wicked in their unbelief, and they could warn people about a Hell prepared for the devil and his angels. Yet they were reluctant to give anyone up to such a fate. They too, lived in tension. If Christ's Kingdom was ever to come, they had to work for it, long for it, and pray for it, continually and earnestly. The more they discovered of the glory of the light of Christ the more intolerable the darkness that seemed to prevail over so much of the world's life. It was to them sheer tragedy that so many seemed to be perishing in a world where Christ had died for all. Woe to them if they did not preach the Gospel. They pled with people passionately to avoid destroying themselves.

The word we have heard in the Cross and Resurrection of Jesus enables us to share the New Testament mood of tri-umphant certainty. However much evil may seem to triumph, in the end it will be exposed, good will be vindicated, justice will be done, and those whom God has predestinated for himself will be his for ever. Though we rejoice in such hope, however, we cannot avoid the tension that must come with it. The powers of evil have been decisively defeated, and are on their way out, but they are not already so disabled that they cannot threaten goodness and God's will. We ourselves have been placed in this world to watch, pray, and resist.

The fact that Christ has died for all must keep alive in our hearts the same frustration of our desire for universal salvation as Christ himself felt. Certainly Jesus finally called Judas "the son of perdition" and in the end gave him the sop and took control of his actions in a final demonstration of his sovereign will over evil, whatever it might try to do (John 13:27). Yet can we not sense in these final dealings with the man a trace of reluctance, in what was taking place? Was he not giving expression to a sense of tragedy when he said that it would have been better if the wretch had never been born? (Matt 26:24). We may think out with the logic of our human minds a doctrine that some are destined from before the world to eternal damnation, but we are not to be blamed if with our hearts we yearn for the salvation of all.

A Confession of Experience and Devotion

When Jesus abruptly challenged the Twelve, *"will you also go away?"* it was a test of the strength of their faith and staying power. The question came as a shock to Peter. He had begun to feel that somehow his true destiny as a human being lay in his future with this man. His life had begun to be controlled only by the desire to serve him and win his approval. His commitment to Jesus had been so whole-hearted that the thought of leaving him had never entered his mind. Even the faint suggestion of it seemed to threaten the bereavement of everything that had now in his service made life worthwhile. So much had he found in this man's friendship and fellowship that now without him life would be dark, empty, hopeless indeed. *"Lord, to whom shall we go? You have the words of eternal life; and we have believed, and have come to know, that you are the Holy One of God."*

Throughout the Gospels there are several notable confessions of faith, affirmations of belief which seemed to rise out of a sudden illumination of mind, or some deep immediate impression, which certain people received, as they met and talked to Jesus. We can put in this category, for example, the confessions made by John the Baptist and other disciples during the early days of their encounter with Jesus, and that made by Peter himself at Caesarea Philippi (cf. 1:34, 1:41, 1:49, Matt. 16:16).

We must however notice that Peter's confession here can be described even more aptly as a confession of experience and devotion. It is an expression not simply of what he has seen in

Jesus in any one momentary exchange or encounter, but of the conviction that has developed within his mind and heart through continuous experience over weeks and months.

The form in which he words his confession is to be noted: "*We have believed, and have come to know, that you are the Holy One of God.*" "Knowledge", observes Hoskyns at this point, "is intensified and permanent belief that was not yet passed into sight." Here we have from Peter indeed the kind of confession given by Polycarp, the aged Bishop of Smyrna, who when he was being dragged into the arena and ordered to blaspheme Christ, said "Eighty and six years have I served him nor hath he ever done me wrong. How can I blaspheme my King and Saviour?"

Possibly the evangelist means us, as we read through this chapter to notice a connection between the experience undergone by the disciples in their previous night's sea-adventure, and this confession of their faith and devotion. After all, that incident was marked by both a "seeing" of Jesus (when they were confronted by the sudden theophany on the waters) and an experience of his power to deliver them from, and see them through, their life's difficulties. Jesus' question and Peter's answer seen in this light, bring out the lesson that such experiences and trials as they went through that night, can serve to strengthen both our vision and our devotion.

Peter in his confession affirms the incomparability and finality of what Jesus brings to us in his person and his teaching. Nowhere else is it imaginable that anyone can find what is to be found in him! He stands unsurpassable, inspiring the awe, reverence and adoration, that belong to God alone, utterly different and apart from all of us even though he is undoubtedly one of us – the Holy One of God!

How did he know, and what right had he, to make such an affirmation? Certainly he had not worked it out on a demonstrable basis. In his small corner of the world he had had no contact with what the other religious faiths or philosophies of the wider world bring to their adherents. In his affirmation of the incomparability of Jesus he was of course simply re-echoing what Jesus was continually saying about himself. He was giving genuine expression to a conviction that he felt inevitable.

Peter did not attribute his exalted belief about Jesus to any remarkable traits of human character, or qualities of heart, mind, and soul, but rather to the fact that Jesus had and spoke *"the words of eternal life"*. He did not mean that his teaching brought us satisfying proof or authoritative information about "eternal life", or even promised it. He meant that his speaking conveyed it. Jesus himself had lived that eternal life with God before the foundation of the world. He had now brought it with him to earth, and he shared it with his disciples when he spoke his words, gave them forgiveness, and the knowledge of God. "This is eternal life that they should know thee the only true God, and Jesus Christ whom thou hast sent" (John 17:3).

Do we ourselves not have the same opportunity as Peter and the other disciples of hearing these *"words of eternal life"*? When Peter wrote his Epistle he invited his readers to listen for them. He spoke of our being born again by the Resurrection of Christ from the dead, and then he explained how this new-life came: "You have been born anew, not of perishable seed but of imperishable, through the living and abiding word of God . . . That word is the good news which was preached to you." (1 Pet. 1:3 and 23 – 5). We hear them today when hungry in our hearts for more than this world can give us we sit and listen to the words of the preacher offering us Christ and his forgiveness, and thus opening up the Kingdom of God to us, opening up heaven to us where he himself is there with the Father. He is the only Son of God who is there, the only Holy One of God – to whom else can we go?

CHAPTER 19

JESUS UNDER CONSTRAINT
John 7:1 – 10

7 After this Jesus went about in Galilee; he would not go about in Judaea, because the Jews sought to kill him. ²Now the Jews' feast of Tabernacles was at hand. ³So his brothers said to him, "Leave here and go to Judaea, that your disciples may see the works you are doing. ⁴For no man works in secret if he seeks to be known openly. If you do these things, show yourself to the world." ⁵For even his brothers did not believe in him. ⁶Jesus said to them, "My time has not yet come, but your time is always here. ⁷The world cannot hate you, but it hates me because I testify of it that its works are evil. ⁸Go to the feast yourselves; I am not going up to the feast, for my time has not yet fully come." ⁹So saying, he remained in Galilee.

10 But after his brothers had gone up to the feast, then he also went up, not publicly but in private.

People were now talking about him everywhere and wondering – what next? Some still admired him; many had doubts and suspicions. In Judaea, where it was now dangerous to express open support for him, the authorities were waiting to trap him.

Since *his brothers did not believe in him* we can understand how acute the situation was for him at home. They hated the local gossip, and the questions they had at times to face. They were beginning to feel that his crusade had gone on too long without result. They thought it a sign of weakness and fear that he now seemed to be avoiding open confrontation. Possibly they fatalistically wished a quick end to the whole sad affair. The

147

approaching feast of Tabernacles seemed to offer a good opportunity of bringing everything to a head. He could now either prove himself, or face what they suspected to be the truth. *"Leave here"*, they challenged him *"and go to Judaea, that your disciples may see the works you are doing. For no man works in secret if he seeks to be known openly"*.

In accusing him of such procrastination and fear, his brothers had shown complete misunderstanding. Jesus at this time was alert, praying, and indeed longing, for the hour to come in which he would be able to enter finally into the last stage of his life on earth, to *show himself to the world* as his brothers were demanding, to incur its bitter hatred, and yield himself to death at its hands. In seeking to answer their accusation he sought to justify himself with a remark that was deliberately enigmatic. Though his brothers would not understand immediately, he knew they would later remember what he said and then see the truth to which they had been so blind. *"My time has not yet come"* he said *"but your time is always here. The world cannot hate you, but it hates me because I testify of it that its works are evil."*

In the light of our knowledge of how events unfolded we can understand what he meant by these words. He himself when he was baptized in the Jordan had deliberately chosen to narrow his life down to one restricted path as he moved towards what the Cross would bring him at the time chosen by the Father. He had then at the Jordan made an appointment with the loneliness, humiliation and suffering which would come to fulfilment in his death when the world would express its hatred of him. Now at this stage in his life he felt himself driven on by a slow relentless pressure towards that "hour". "How I am constrained until it is accomplished!" he had said (Luke 12.50) as he gave expression to the inner constraint that now dominated his life.

Jesus now compares the narrow way he has to travel with the way of freedom that was open to his brothers in their choice of path. Within the life of mankind he recognized that God had made "a time for every matter under heaven" and "everything beautiful in its time" (Eccl. 3:1, 11). How varied were these "times" selected by God in working out the lives of ordinary men and women on this earth! He looked around him at other people who could find simple and satisfying pleasure in daily work, healthy recreation, simple cultural pursuits and family life, and he thought about the contrast between them and himself. How much they could often themselves plan and choose within all those possibilities open to them! Had he himself not wished at times for freedom from the one dominating constraint that had so hemmed him in? *"My time has not yet come"*, he said to his brothers, *"but your time is always here."*

The New Testament often underlines the contrast, here brought out by Jesus himself, between what he took on himself for our sakes when he went to the Cross, and what he gives us in exchange. He was made "sin" for us that we might be given his righteousness (2 Cor. 5:21). He became poor that we might be made rich (2 Cor. 8:9). He took our chastisement that we might have peace, our sickness that we might have health (Matt. 8:17). Here from his own lips we have another of these contrasts between the narrow restriction of the way he has to choose for himself, and the breadth of inheritance he offers up for those for whom he dies. Paul in one place tries to give full expression to this breadth: "All things are yours, whether . . . the world or life or death or the present or the future, all are yours" (1 Cor. 3:21 – 2).

His sense of isolation seemed completely to take him over at this point. We are meant to notice how anxious he was to detach himself publicly from any suspicion of yielding to family pressure in deciding the course of his public ministry. His gentle word of caution to his mother at the wedding at Cana had already revealed his anxiety to work free from such pressure. Now, much more bluntly he resists the anxiety of his brothers to push him their way. *"Go to the feast yourselves. I am not going up."*

Yet the constraint under which the will of God had placed him, later took him up *not publicly but in private*. There can be little doubt that after their recent dramatic confession of inseparable loyalty to him, his disciples were then with him, in the background. The sight of them there also willingly sharing something of his isolation from the world of their day and of the constraint that was driving him towards his Cross is a reminder to us that our own discipleship can at times demand the sacrifice of the very liberty he has died to win us. Paul who repeatedly insists in his letters to the Corinthians "All things are lawful" (1 Cor. 10:23), also sets before us in himself the perfect example of how to deny ourselves this very freedom. "For the love of Christ controls us, because we are convinced that one has died for all; therefore all have died. And he died for all, that those who live might live no longer for themselves, but for him who for their sake died and was raised" (2 Cor. 5:14 – 15).

CHAPTER 20

THE GREAT CONTROVERSY

There are many details within the account of the long
controversy in the Temple at the feast of Tabernacles which
cannot be brought within the scope and purpose of this present
exposition. We have therefore divided the whole account of it
into four sections. We have used the first section to illustrate
the mood and development of the whole controversy, using
the part as an example of the whole. Then we have selected,
for more detailed treatment, and each within its own context,
three important words of Jesus, which appear consecutively,
and which are outstanding in the midst of the whole
discussion. The text is printed in continuity so that the reader
can read it through and note the connections.

Jesus on the Attack

John 7:11 –36

The Jews were looking for him at the feast, and saying,
"Where is he?" [12]And there was much muttering about
him among the people. While some said, "He is a good
man," others said, "No, he is leading the people
astray." [13]Yet for fear of the Jews no one spoke openly of
him.

14 About the middle of the feast Jesus went up into the
temple and taught. [5]The Jews marvelled at it, saying,
"How is it that this man has learning, when he has never
studied?" [16]So Jesus answered them, "My teaching is
not mine, but his who sent me; [17]if any man's will is to
do his will, he shall know whether the teaching is from
God or whether I am speaking on my own authority.

151

[18]He who speaks on his own authority seeks his own glory; but he who seeks the glory of him who sent him is true, and in him there is no falsehood. [19]Did not Moses give you the law? Yet none of you keeps the law. Why do you seek to kill me?" [20]The people answered, "You have a demon! Who is seeking to kill you?" [21] Jesus answered them, "I did one deed, and you all marvel at it. [22]Moses gave you circumcision (not that it is from Moses, but from the fathers), and you circumcise a man upon the sabbath. [23]If on the sabbath a man receives circumcision, so that the law of Moses may not be broken, are you angry with me because on the sabbath I made a man's whole body well? [24]Do not judge by appearances, but judge with right judgement."

25 Some of the people of Jerusalem therefore said, "Is not this the man whom they seek to kill? [26]And here he is, speaking openly, and they say nothing to him! Can it be that the authorities really know that this is the Christ? [27]Yet we know where this man comes from; and when the Christ appears, no one will know where he comes from." [28]So Jesus proclaimed, as he taught in the temple, "You know me, and you know where I come from? But I have not come of my own accord; he who sent me is true, and him you do not know. [29]I know him, for I come from him, and he sent me." [30]So they sought to arrest him; but no one laid hands on him, because his hour had not yet come. [31]Yet many of the people believed in him; they said, "When the Christ appears, will he do more signs than this man has done?"

32The Parisees heard the crowd thus muttering about him, and the chief priests and Pharisees sent officers to arrest him. [33]Jesus then said, "I shall be with you a little longer, and then I go to him who sent me; [34]you will seek me and you will not find me; where I am you cannot come." [35]The Jews said to one another, "Where does this man intend to go that we shall not find him? Does he intend to go to the Dispersion among the Greeks and teach the Greeks? [36]What does he mean by saying, 'You will seek me and you will not find me,' and, 'Where I am you cannot come'?"

The discussion began immediately Jesus arrived, and it went on day after day. We find him moving around, confronting different groups here and there. Sometimes he lifts up his voice and addresses the whole assembly around him. The mood of his hearers varies. People around him at the beginning are anxious, questioning and suspicious. As the days pass the atmosphere grows more tense and hostile.

He sets the discussion in motion with a supremely confident affirmation of the undeniable truth of his teaching and the convincing authority with which it was always being given. It came from God. *"My teaching is not mine, but his who sent me."* He was always certain that as he spoke, God the Father spoke too (cf. 8:14, 5:34ff.).

He believed that, whether or not it produced any immediate response, his voice would be always resonant with the same power as could heal the sick, open blind eyes, and raise the dead. He was convinced, therefore, that his ministry among this crowd before him was going to reveal whether people were for or against God. If heart and mind were open and inclined to the truth, any hearer would respond and learn from him: *"if any man's will is to do his will, he shall know"*. If any man responded otherwise he would inevitably become perplexed, mystified and hardened into an attitude of deadly enmity.

He warned them about the hatred he had already discerned in their reaction to the healing of the impotent man at the Pool on the Sabbath day. He challenged them to be honest about the desire that was in their hearts to kill him. As if to save them from their folly he tried to show them that they could find no real support for their attitude in the Law of Moses. A notable pause in their increasing hostility seems to take place towards the end of the feast when Jesus finds himself surrounded by a group of people who seem ready to believe in him, but these very people soon find his attempt to help them towards true faith insulting, react with open abuse and then take up stones in an attempt to kill him on the spot (8:48, 59).

The reader of the whole discourse will notice that much of the discussion is about Jesus' own personal origin. His attackers had objected to his claim to be the Christ because they knew where he came from, and *"when Christ appears no one will know where he comes from"* (v.27 cf. 6:41ff). Jesus insists that his personal origin must remain a mystery about which in their present state of mind they can know nothing. Moreover, ironically, he provokes and puzzles them by warning them that in their present state of mind his future destiny will remain as unknown to them as his origin. Where he goes, they *"cannot come"*. They will die in their sins (7:34, 8:14, 21). Referring to their own origins, his conclusion is that since they do not recognize the Father from whom he has come, they have forsaken the Fatherhood of God, and made the devil their father (8:42 – 4).

We are meant to notice the decisive part this controversy plays within John's Gospel, in bringing Jesus to his death. During these several days of teaching the whole climate of public opinion in Jerusalem is being altered. People are beginning to think themselves disillusioned with him, and are wondering whether their leaders have had some justification for the judgement they have made. The Pharisees have become much more confident that, possibly before the coming Passover, they will have him in their power. Yet it is Jesus himself who brings about this movement of events. Throughout the Feast, as everywhere else in the Gospel of John, he shows himself regally in control of everything that happens around him as he moves towards the Cross. He lays down his own life. No one takes it from him (10:17 – 18). He initiates the controversy, controls it at every juncture, decides the theme and the course of the discussion, increases or moderates the tension, provokes reaction.

It is to be noted that he exercises his complete command and control of the events around him by his Word. He does no miracle during this momentous week. He makes no political manoeuvre, organizes no protest of any kind. It is simply by his speaking, pleading, teaching, warning, inviting, proclaiming, that he plays his decisive part in moving public affairs on to the course God has destined them to take. Here is the perfect illustration of how God's Word goes forth from his mouth into human history to accomplish his will (cf. Isa. 55:10 – 11). Moreover the theme of his teaching in this decisive week is, as usual in this Gospel, almost entirely himself. He speaks of who he is, where he has come from, what he has come to do and where he is going. This is how he fulfils the challenge laid down by his brothers to "show himself to the world" so that the world could make its final decision about him. The teaching he gives here is not consciously directed in any way towards public affairs, or the details of personal ethics. There is no prophetic call for social justice, nothing directly "anti-establishment". These two chapters are difficult to fit into any theory that what brought Jesus to the Cross was primarily his revolutionary teaching about our moral standards, his devastating criticism of our earthly social structures, or his radical views about the distribution of wealth. What stirred the anger of his enemies, provoked their madness, and made them determined to crucify him was simply – Himself.

In taking note of Jesus' attacking initiative we must not, however, fail to remember that here he was confronting the city over which at this very time he wept. These were the people he continually yearned to win for himself (cf. Luke 19:41). We must not therefore underestimate in any way the genuineness of the appeals with which this controversy is punctuated, nor the suffering he felt under the continual rejection which he had to face.

The Offer of Life

John 7:37 – 52

37 On the last day of the feast, the great day, Jesus stood up and proclaimed, "If any one thirst, let him come to me and drink. ³⁸He who believes in me, as the scripture has said, 'Out of his heart shall flow rivers of living water.'" ³⁹Now this he said about the Spirit, which those who believed in him were to receive; for as yet the Spirit had not been given, because Jesus was not yet glorified.

40 When they heard these words, some of the people said, "This is really the prophet." ⁴¹Others said, "This is the Christ." But some said, "Is the Christ to come from Galilee? ⁴²Has not the scripture said that the Christ is descended from David, and comes from

Bethlehem, the village where David was?" ⁴³So there
was a division among the people over him. ⁴⁴Some of
them wanted to arrest him, but no one laid hands on
him.

45 The officers then went back to the chief priests and
Pharisees, who said to them, "Why did you not bring
him?" ⁴⁶The officers answered, "No man ever spoke
like this man!" ⁴⁷The Pharisees answered them, "Are
you led astray, you also? ⁴⁸Have any of the authorities
or of the Pharisees believed in him?" ⁴⁹But this crowd,
who do not know the law, are accursed." ⁵⁰Nicodemus,
who had gone to him before, and who was one of them,
said to them, ⁵¹"Does our law judge a man without first
giving him a hearing and learning what he does?"
⁵²They replied, "Are you from Galilee too? Search and
you will see that no prophet is to rise from Galilee."

The setting was picturesque and the occasion dramatic.
Throughout much of the feast, the thought of those present
was directed to the desert wanderings of the Children of Israel,
and to incidents on their way, such as Moses' striking of the
Rock to bring them water. The worshippers were reminded
too, of certain prophetic texts which promised that in the days
of the Messiah such refreshing waters would marvellously
flow again. Zechariah, for example, had made the promise
that one day "living waters shall flow out of Jerusalem", and
Ezekiel had seen a river flow from the rock underneath the
altar of the Temple (cf.Zec. 14:8, Ezek. 47:1ff.). On each of
the seven days of the feast the people went in procession from
the Temple down to the fountain which supplied the Pool of
Siloam where the priest filled a golden vase from the running
water, and the choir sang verses from the twelfth chapter of
Isaiah. They carried the vase back to the Temple through the
Watergate, proceeded round the altar singing prayers from
the end of the hundred and eighteenth Psalm, then they
poured the water over the altar.

The eighth day, *the last day of the feast*, however, was a day of
waiting. The crowd gathered in the Temple courts and there
was silence. The devout worshippers there then prayed for the
great day to come when all the hope of Israel would be

fulfilled. Some indeed expected to see the promised miracle of a fountain of running water burst open in the Temple courts. It was this solemn moment that Jesus chose for one of his great acts of self-proclamation, raising his voice so that all could hear: *"If any one thirst, let him come to me and drink. He who believes in me, as the scripture has said, 'Out of his heart shall flow rivers of living water'."* Here and now, as Moses had brought forth rivers of living water from the Rock, was their Messiah offering himself as the true River of Life (Rev. 22:1), the source from which his people can from now on draw, and give to the whole world.

The disciples who report this incident to us explain that Jesus spoke these words chiefly as a promise, and was referring to the Holy Spirit which, when he was later glorified, he poured out on the Church (v.39). His dramatic call, however, at the time of its utterance was as eloquent and emphatic a claim as he could have made, to be the Messiah in whom his people were meant to find and enjoy their true destiny.

It is today therefore, now that the Holy Spirit has been given in its fullness, that these words can be heard by us with even more challenging force than they had when first spoken. We can hear them as an appeal to us to re-assess what life has brought to us. We note that it was on the *"last . . . the great day"* – at the climax and crisis of their ancient feast – that Israel, year after year, expecting so much, found their earthly hopes still unfulfilled. So we, too, have our own crises of disappointment and disillusionment, when we begin to know how unsatisfying the routine of life has been, and how much we really *thirst*. Earthly pleasure, or wealth, or success, can suddenly prove what seems a basic emptiness. Life's inevitable changes, chances and bereavements can suddenly seem to rob us of what has been truly good and worthy. What comes to us through our religious devotion and worship, however magnificent the ritual, however fervent the enthusiasm, can leave us still with a longing for something more real and satisfying. It is especially at these times that we can hear this voice assuring us that in place of all the "broken cisterns that can hold no water", the "fountain of living waters" (Jer. 2:13) is full and marvellously refreshing if we will only now come to him, drink, and share what we have been given with a needy and perishing world.

If anything Jesus ever did was deliberately calculated to be sensational it was to make his public call at this time. It was carefully prepared for, and must have been deeply and genuinely impressive. No one could have escaped either the meaning of the action or the strength of the claim. No doubt he expected some sign that his words had gone home. Certainly some were moved to voice their opinions: *"This is really the prophet"* . . . *"This is the Christ."* Yet, what finally happened proved in the end simply to be the beginning of a further controversy: *"So there was a division among the people over him."*

The Offer of Light

John 8:12 – 30

12 Again Jesus spoke to them, saying, "I am the light of the world; he who follows me will not walk in darkness, but will have the light of life." [13]The Pharisees then said to him, "You are bearing witness to yourself; your testimony is not true." [14]Jesus answered, "Even if I do bear witness to myself, my testimony is true, for I know whence I have come and whither I am going, but you do not know whence I come or whither I am going. [15]You judge according to the flesh, I judge no one. [16]Yet even if I do judge, my judgement is true, for it is not I alone that judge, but I and he who sent me. [17]In your law it is written that the testimony of two men is true; [18]I bear witness to myself, and the Father who sent me bears witness to me." [19]They said to him therefore, "Where is your Father?" Jesus answered, "You know neither me nor my Father; if you knew me, you would know my Father also." [20]These words he spoke in the treasury, as he taught in the temple; but no one arrested him, because his hour had not yet come.

21 Again he said to them, "I go away, and you will seek me and die in your sin; where I am going, you cannot come." [22]Then said the Jews, "Will he kill himself, since he says, 'Where I am going, you cannot

come'?" [23]He said to them, "You are from below, I am
from above; you are of this world, I am not of this world.
[24]I told you that you would die in your sins, for you will
die in your sins unless you believe that I am he." [25]They
said to him, "Who are you?" Jesus said to them, "Even
what I have told you from the beginning. [26]I have much
to say about you and much to judge; but he who sent me
is true, and I declare to the world what I have heard from
him." [27]They did not understand that he spoke to them
of the Father. [28]So Jesus said, "When you have lifted up
the Son of man, then you will know that I am he, and that
I do nothing on my own authority but speak thus as the
Father taught me. [29]And he who sent me is with me; he
has not left me alone, for I always do what is pleasing to
him." [30]As he spoke thus, many believed in him.

Alongside the celebration involving the drawing of water
there was also a feast of lights during the Tabernacles week. It
involved the lighting of the Golden Candlestick in the Court of
the Women. The Jews thus remembered that during their
wanderings in the wilderness there was the marvellous pillar
of fire to lead them, as well as the marvellous flow of water to
refresh them. They always thought of God as one who gives
light alongside of life. "For with thee is the fountain of life; in
thy light do we see light" (Ps. 36:9 cf. John 1:4). A second
dramatic appeal was made therefore by Jesus in the course of
the celebration; *"I am the light of the world: he who follows me shall
not walk in darkness, but will have the light of life"*.
If we read the many lamentations, dirges, and psalms of
complaint scattered throughout the literature of the Old
Testament we will be given a trustworthy impression of what
men and women in that ancient world felt as they faced the
darkness that surrounds our human life. They felt often
indeed hemmed in by it, and they feared the cruel and hostile
nature of much that it enshrouded. We hear them crying and
questioning out of a perplexity and pain that they feel at times
to be incurable. Why these ghastly horrors of war, terrorism
and natural disaster – "death entering the windows of their
homes, the dead bodies of men fallen like dung upon the open
fields, like sheaves before the reaper"? It was all so modern,

and in their case there was "none to gather up" the corpses! (cf. Jer. 9:21 – 2) Why all this? And why the unfairness and injustice of it all? Where is the meaning of life to be found in the midst of all its vanities, corruption and uncertainties? How and when is God going to put everything right, and show that everything has been put right? Of course they were able to endure and overcome, often with triumphant and, indeed, radiant faith, for even when they felt they had no direct answer to their questionings, the Word of God was a light to their path and a lamp to their feet. (Ps. 119:105). How much praise for triumph, deliverance and revelation there is in the same literature that so frankly faces up to the darkness!.

It is in this context that we are meant to assess and understand the promise of Jesus. We "*shall not walk in darkness*". Of course the darkness is still there around us, sinister and impenetrable in places, but the balance has swung entirely in favour of the light. We still have a few short dirges, lamentations and complaints in the New Testament – especially in the Book of Revelation – but they are brief and limited. The writer to the Hebrews puts it in perspective. He *almost* complains: "We do not yet see everything in subjection to him." There are many disasters and wars, many prayers and questions still unanswered, many longings still to be stifled. "But", he adds, "we see Jesus, who for a little while was made lower than the angels, crowned with glory and honour!" (Heb. 2:8 – 9). Here is true light, far-reaching, promising and clear. It is "*the light of life*". Though it does not offer a quick solution to our intellectual problems, does not make it easy to indulge in continual triumphalism, it enables us to see enough of the purpose and meaning of life to have a wide open field of opportunity and personal responsibility in the service of God, of whose guidance and friendship we can be sure.

It is a light that gives itself to those who obey it. It is "*he who follows me*" who has the light. The gift which was celebrated in the feast of Tabernacles was that of a light which went on the move, ahead, choosing the direction and the way for God's people. To live in it they had to keep up with it. It was those who failed to follow who were left in darkness. We cannot control or refract this light, bending its rays in our self-chosen directions. We have to go where it is to be found. As Jesus himself later said: "If any one serves me, he must follow me, and where I am, there shall my servant be also" (John 12:26).

We are meant to take notice of the sweeping universality and unqualified breadth of his claim. He speaks of only *one* and claims to be it: "*the light of the world*". He is not one among others. If others before him had some light, it must have been *his* light they saw. He was and is the one towards whom in their own darkness they were all moving. Whatever beams of wisdom and truth they had, derived from him. All is darkness that does not acknowledge him. He who looks to him shall see everything that matters in the realm of ultimate truth.

The Light Shines in Darkness

At the point at which Jesus utters his claim to be the "light of the world" one of the latest editions of the Gospel of John inserted a story about Jesus which is obviously genuine, but which had found no final place within any of the other Gospels. It was inserted at this point because it illustrates how in Jesus the light, as it shines into the darkness of our human minds, exposes and repels hypocrisy and cleanses from sin.

John 7:53 – 8:11

7 ⁵³They went each to his own house, 8 ¹but Jesus went to the Mount of Olives. ²Early in the morning he came again to the temple; all the people came to him, and he sat down and taught them. ³The scribes and the Pharisees brought a woman who had been caught in adultery, and placing her in the midst ⁴they said to him, "Teacher, this woman has been caught in the act of adultery. ⁵Now in the law Moses commanded us to stone such. What do you say about her?" ⁶This they said to test him, that they might have some charge to bring against him. Jesus bent down and wrote with his finger on the ground. ⁷And as they continued to ask him, he stood up and said to them, "Let him who is without sin among you be the first to throw a stone at her." ⁸And once more he bent down and wrote with his finger on the ground. ⁹But when they heard it, they went away, one

by one, beginning with the eldest, and Jesus was left alone with the woman standing before him. ¹⁰Jesus looked up and said to her, "Woman, where are they? Has no one condemned you?" ¹¹She said, "No one, Lord." And Jesus said, "Neither do I condemn you; go, and do not sin again."

The scribes and Pharisees had not a shade of doubt, nor a qualm of conscience, in their minds when they brought this woman to Jesus for his judgement. She had been caught in the act, and it was an anti-social act of the most serious nature. In the Ten Commandments it is listed along with murder and stealing as a sin which society must not tolerate, and the prescribed punishment ordered by Moses in this case was death. *"Moses commanded us to stone such."* No doubt they themselves hated the task of executing the sentence in cold blood, but they were the responsible guardians of public decency and order, and they were prepared to do it. They cared that their children around them should grow up in a healthy society where marriage was held in honour.

The thought, however, came to them: Why not make this a test case in their fight against Jesus? They had no doubt about the verdict they themselves had passed, but they were in real doubt about Jesus' loyalty to this law. He had once said something about lustful thoughts being as bad as adultery.

Did this mean that the outward behaviour of people did not matter, and that adulterers were to be tolerated as being no more dangerous than people who sinned only with the mind? He had made suggestions about the possibility of publicans and harlots entering the Kingdom of God – and there were stories of him having dealings with women of bad repute. They would use this opportunity of putting him to the test in public: *"Teacher, this woman has been caught in the act of adultery . . . What do you say about her?"* – They had the stones in their hands, and they were confident of the outcome.

They had hoped that their sudden intrusion would bring about a dramatic and devastating public exposure of Jesus in the eyes of the public around him. Instead, they were completely taken aback at what happened. It was they who, in the sudden publicity they had brought on themsleves, began to feel stupidly awkward just when they had hoped to be so triumphant. Jesus, instead, was calm, confident and silent for a while. No doubt to prolong the silence he bent down and wrote with his finger in the sand. When they had begun to grow even more uneasy with the situation they had so unwittingly created, *he stood up and said to them "Let him who is without sin among you be the first to throw a stone at her"*, and he again bent down and wrote on the ground.

It is the complete collapse of their self-confidence in the presence of Jesus that we are meant to notice. Undoubtedly when they took the woman so boldly before him they thought they knew enough about themselves, about life, and about Jesus, to see this whole case through. But then when they entered his presence the light of his truth began to penetrate their consciences, and when they heard his challenge to face what each of them now saw himself to be, *"they went away, one by one, beginning with the eldest"*. All their sham self-certainty gone! They had no moral self-defence left. They found themselves unable to tolerate the light of his truth. To save their pride and protect their false self-image which had been their comfortable disguise, they felt they had to get away from him as quickly as possible – back to the darkness from which they had come. It is significant that the darkness to which they return is the very darkness under cover of which they will now join in the plot to quench the light that has so exposed them to themselves.

And now the world of difference between them and the woman they had brought with them becomes clear. Of course the public exhibition of her guilt had been at first like a torture to her, and possibly they had had to drag her along with them. But something happened to her as well as to them during that strange silence in the presence of Jesus, as he had stooped down to write on the ground. In contrast to the men, the woman seems to have found herself accepted and at home with him. She made no attempt to leave him, till *Jesus looked up and said to her, "Woman, where are they? Has no one condemned you?" She said, "No one, Lord." And Jesus said, "Neither do I condemn you; go and do not sin again."*

We need not imagine that his word *"neither do I condemn you"* was a condonation of her sin. She herself had already, without any attempt at self-defence, had her sin fully exposed and condemned in his presence. There was no need for anything more to be said about it. Moreover, the fact that she alone made no attempt to leave his presence means that she accepted the condemnation, that she no longer wants to return to that darkness which she has now given up for ever. A prominent Biblical scholar of a former generation once published an eloquent and persuasive sermon suggesting that the word "*go and sin no more*" was an expression of trust rather than a stern threat. She went, knowing that he trusted her. The contrast between herself and those who hauled her before him is complete. Our human destiny is determined by how each one of us reacts when his light falls upon us.

The Offer of Freedom

John 8:30 – 59

30 As he spoke thus, many believed in him.

31 Jesus then said to the Jews who had believed in him, "If you continue in my word, you are truly my disciples, ³²and you will know the truth, and the truth will make you free." ³³They answered him, "We are descendants of Abraham, and have never been in bondage to anyone. How is it that you say, 'You will be made free'?"

34 Jesus answered them, "Truly, truly, I say to you, every one who commits sin is a slave to sin. ³⁵The slave does not continue in the house for ever; the son continues for ever. ³⁶So if the Son makes you free, you will be free indeed. ³⁷I know that you are descendants of Abraham; yet you seek to kill me, because my word finds no place in you. ³⁸I speak of what I have seen with my Father, and you do what you have heard from your father."

39 They answered him, "Abraham is our father". Jesus said to them, "If you were Abraham's children, you would do what Abraham did, ⁴⁰but now you seek to kill me, a man who has told you the truth which I heard from God; this is not what Abraham did. ⁴¹You do what your father did." They said to him, "We were not born

of fornication; we have one Father, even God." [42]Jesus said to them, "If God were your Father, you would love me, for I proceeded and came forth from God; I came not of my own accord, but he sent me. [43]Why do you not understand what I say? It is because you cannot bear to hear my word. [44]You are of your father the devil, and your will is to do your father's desires. He was a murderer from the beginning, and has nothing to do with the truth, because there is no truth in him. When he lies, he speaks according to his own nature, for he is a liar and the father of lies. [45]But, because I tell the truth, you do not believe me. [46]Which of you convicts me of sin? If I tell the truth, why do you not believe me? [47]He who is of God hears the words of God; the reason why you do not hear them is that you are not of God."

48 The Jews answered him, "Are we not right in saying that you are a Samaritan and have a demon?" [49]Jesus answered, "I have not a demon; but I honour my Father, and you dishonour me. [50]Yet I do not seek my own glory; there is One who seeks it and he will be the judge. [51]Truly, truly, I say to you, if any one keeps my word, he will never see death." [52]The Jews said to him, "Now we know that you have a demon. Abraham died, as did the prophets; and you say, 'If any one keeps my word, he will never taste death.' [53]Are you greater than our father Abraham, who died? And the prophets died! Who do you claim to be?" [54]Jesus answered, If I glorify myself, my glory is nothing; it is my Father who glorifies me, of whom you say that he is your God. [55]But you have not known him; I know him. If I said, I do not know him, I should be a liar like you; but I do know him and I keep his word. [56]Your father Abraham rejoiced that he was to see my day; he saw it and was glad." [57]The Jews then said to him, "You are not yet fifty years old, and have you seen Abraham?" [58]Jesus said to them, "Truly, truly, I say to you, before Abraham was, I am." [59]So they took up stones to throw at him; but Jesus hid himself, and went out of the temple.

As we have pointed out, suddenly, for a short time, the tone of the debate in the Temple seemed to change. The mood of confrontation gave way to a wave of what seemed to be genuine interest. The evangelist describing the situation says *"many believed in him"*. It is obvious that their hold on what he was giving them was very tentative and slender. Calvin calls their change of attitude simply a "preparation for faith". But Jesus felt it was worthwhile trying to strengthen it. With pastoral concern and his never slackening desire to win people over, he treated those who approached him as genuine inquirers.

He had already given warnings about those who "endure for a while", and when tribulation and persecution arise on account of the word "immediately fall away" (Matt 13:18ff.). He knew only too well therefore, that the wave of interest they were experiencing would soon subside unless he could persuade them to become more open in mind to all his teaching and bring them more fully under his influence. He made it clear to them what entering such commitment would involve. *"If you continue in my word, you are truly my disciples, and you will know the truth, and the truth will make you free."*

The challenge to *"continue in my word"*, of course involves us in a study of his teaching with the same ardent devotion as the Psalmist had for the law when he made it his "meditation all the day". (Ps.119:97). It involves a persevering effort to know and understand the whole of it, refusing to be content with only a partial knowledge of a few selected passages that have caught our approval and imagination, and including those passages that tend to offend and condemn us. We must work out as fully as we can all the implications for our own lives, of obedience. Moreover, we must bring before our minds in this way not only the words of Jesus but his person, and of course the works in which we find him presenting himself to us. The New English Bible brings out this aspect of his exhortation in its translation: *"If you dwell within the revelation I have brought . . . you shall know the truth."* After all, he himself in what he does, is the truth, and the truth, as Hoskyns remarks, "cannot be detached from the figure of flesh and blood which was Jesus".

There can be little doubt that this first piece of advice, with its inevitable orientation to himself, would cause some annoyance among his hearers. The assertion that immediately followed was deliberately even more provocative: "The truth I bring to you *will make you free*" Jesus claimed. It was an accusation that they were all in bondage, and they were angered.

Jesus, of course, was referring to our inner bondage to evil and self-centred ways of thought and behaviour, our bondage to sin. This was the one evil in life which gave him most concern: "What proceeds from the heart" he had said, " . . . defiles a man" (Matt. 15:18). His hearers on their own part should have understood what he was referring to. It was the teaching of their Scriptures, and they prided themselves in their faithfulness to the traditions of their fathers. But their minds had drifted from such truth, and had become almost completely oriented to what was only of immediate secular and social relevance. They interpreted his reference to "freedom" politically. He seemed to be implying that they were at present in bondage to Rome. They reacted immediately to what they took as an insult to their national pride. "*We are descendants of Abraham, and have never been in bondage to anyone. How is it that you say, 'You will be made free'?*"

Jesus seized the invitation to give them an elementary lesson in the truth they had been unwilling to face. His argument is easy to follow. The original source of everything that has blighted our human life is our sin, our deep inward alienation from God. Unless we find true inward freedom, it takes each one of us over, working like an inner power within us forcing us against our own better will into attitudes and habits that degrade us. Nothing in any aspect of our personal or social life can go right while we remain in such bondage to our self-will and inner weaknesses.

There is a warning here especially about the insecurity and transitoriness of the political freedom about which they were boasting. "*The slave does not continue in the house for ever; the son continues for ever.*" Political stability is the privilege only of those who have inwardly accepted the liberation Jesus has offered and thus become themselves sons of God. We can affirm that even a healthy social freedom can be enjoyed only by a people who give full and free place in their midst to the Gospel which produces in the inward heart the liberty of the children of God to which Jesus is here referring. When our country was facing the Second World war one of our leading Churchmen published a little book about the foundations of the freedom we professed to be fighting for. He uttered a plea for the cultivation of the virtues of restraint and discipline that are peculiarly the fruit of the Spirit of Christ, and added the warning "You cannot grow an oak in a flower pot". Only if the Son makes us free can we be "*free indeed*".

With a final rejoinder, Jesus thrust home his point and entered the attack again. These men who had professed themselves so deeply hurt at his accusation, were proving its truth by their very thoughts and attitude. They could not free themselves from the deceiving effects of their inward pride, nor from their completely irrational desire to kill him. The break in the controversy therefore simply opens it up again. The accusations of the Jews grow more insulting, and Jesus himself becomes less and less restrained in his replies. The discussion revolves around Abraham and what it means to be truly his offspring. In the end Jesus who had claimed that Abraham rejoiced to see his day, uttered one of his most majestic and memorable sayings: "*before Abraham was, I am.*" The one who revealed himself to Moses at the Bush when he made all his greatest promises and claims to his people, used the same simple and majestic word to describe his incomparable self (cf. Exod. 3:14, Deut. 32:39, Isa. 43:10).

CHAPTER 21

THE MAN BORN BLIND
John 9:1 – 41

9 As he passed by, he saw a man blind from his birth. ²And his disciples asked him, "Rabbi, who sinned, this man or his parents, that he was born blind?" ³Jesus answered, "It was not that this man sinned, or his parents, but that the works of God might be made manifest in him. ⁴We must work the works of him who sent me, while it is day; night comes, when no one can work. ⁵As long as I am in the world, I am the light of the world." ⁶As he said this, he spat on the ground and made clay of the spittle and annointed the man's eyes with the clay, ⁷saying to him, "Go, wash in the pool of Siloam" (which means Sent). So he went and washed and came back seeing. ⁸The neighbours and those who had seen him before as a beggar, said, "Is not this the man who used to sit and beg?" ⁹Some said, "It is he"; others said, "No, but he is like him." He said, "I am the man." ¹⁰They said to him, "Then how were your eyes opened?" ¹¹He answered, "The man called Jesus made clay and anointed my eyes and said to me, 'Go to Siloam and wash'; so I went and washed and received my sight." ¹²They said to him, "Where is he?" He said, "I do not know."

13 They brought to the Pharisees the man who had formerly been blind. ¹⁴Now it was the sabbath day when Jesus made the clay and opened his eyes. ¹⁵The Pharisees again asked him how he had received his sight. And he said to them, "He put clay on my eyes, and I washed, and I see." ¹⁶Some of the Pharisees said, "This man is not from God, for he does not keep the sabbath."

But others said, "How can a man who is a sinner do such signs?" There was a division among them. [17]So they again said to the blind man, "What do you say about him, since he has opened your eyes?" He said, "He is a prophet."

18 The Jews did not believe that he had been blind and had received his sight, until they called the parents of the man who had received his sight, [19]and asked them, "Is this your son, who you say was born blind? How then does he now see?"[20]His parents answered, "We know that this is our son, and that he was born blind; [21]but how he now sees we do not know, nor do we know who opened his eyes. Ask him; he is of age, he will speak for himself." [22]His parents said this because they feared the Jews, for the Jews had already agreed that if any one should confess him to be Christ, he was to be put out of the synagogue. [23]Therefore his parents said, "He is of age, ask him."

24 So for the second time they called the man who had been blind, and said to him, "Give God the praise; we know that this man is a sinner." [25]He answered, "Whether he is a sinner, I do not know; one thing I know, that though I was blind, now I see." [26]They said to him, "What did he do to you? How did he open your eyes?" [27]He answered them, "I have told you already, and you would not listen. Why do you want to hear it again? Do you too want to become his disciples?" [28]And they reviled him, saying, "You are his disciple, but we are disciples of Moses. [29]We know that God has spoken to Moses, but as for this man, we do not know where he comes from." [30]The man answered, "Why, this is a marvel! You do not know where he comes from and yet he opened my eyes. [31]We know that God does not listen to sinners, but if any one is a worshipper of God and does his will, God listens to him. [32]Never since the world began has it been heard that any one opened the eyes of a man born blind. [33]If this man were not from God, he could do nothing." [34]They answered him, "You were born in utter sin, and would you teach us?" And they cast him out.

35Jesus heard that they had cast him out, and having found him he said, "Do you believe in the Son of man?" ³⁶He answered, "And who is he, sir, that I may believe in him?" ³⁷Jesus said to him, "You have seen him, and it is he who speaks to you." ³⁸He said, "Lord, I believe"; and he worshipped him. ³⁹Jesus said, "For judgement I came into this world, that those who do not see may see, and that those who see may become blind." ⁴⁰Some of the Pharisees near him heard this, and they said to him, "Are we also blind?" ⁴¹Jesus said to them, "If you were blind, you would have no guilt; but now that you say, 'We see,' your guilt remains."

A Plea for Fresh Vision and Action

It is said of Queen Marie Antoinette that on one of her important royal processions through Paris, she gave orders that where she was going, the streets should be cleared of all the poor or deformed beggars who usually held their stances in the area. She did not want to be made to feel uncomfortable or sorrowful on a great occasion. In the days of Jesus, however, people passing through the streets on their way to market, temple, place of work or political assembly could not escape being confronted, sometimes dramatically and rudely by the contents of their impoverished slum hovels, laid out before them – helpless people with paralysis, ugly deformities, and wasting sicknesses; sometimes due to poverty, sometimes to neglect and ignorance, sometimes to their birth; all reminders of an immense amount of human suffering.

Of course the sight continually plagued the minds of sensitive people and formed a large persistent and dark shadow in the background of their thought as they tried to figure out what life was all about. They gave alms no doubt generously, but they were at times disturbed by inner questioning – especially if they knew some of the intimate details and tragic circumstances of some of the cases around them. The disciples were this day discussing the obvious poverty and the pathetic misery of this *"man blind from his birth"* whom Jesus himself had noticed. They felt certain that his suffering was due to sin. Was it possible that he was suffering for the sins of his parents? Or was it possible that the man himself in a previous life could have committed a grievous damaging sin? They took the problem to Jesus: *Rabbi who sinned?*

The final answer that Jesus gave to their question was of course to heal the man before them, and change the whole human situation, but before he did so he rebuked them. Their well intentioned but fruitless discussion, their hopeless acceptance of things as they are, revealed the shortness of vision, the callous despair and darkness of mind, that he had come to abolish. He pled with them to take a new look at the situation before them, to see that with his own presence now in their midst, a new age had dawned on the world, tranforming our ways of looking at life and our response to all the problems presented to us by its evils and injustices. He therefore lifted up the whole discussion to this entirely new level: "*It was not that this man sinned or his parents, but that the works of God might be made manifest in him. We must work the works of him who sent me, while it is day; night comes, when no man can work. As long as I am in the world, I am the light of the world.*"

There is urgency in his appeal. At this time in his life he had not long to live – perhaps only a week or two. His death had been plotted. His supporters were falling away. He likens himself here to someone approaching the evening of life with only a short span of daylight left. Therefore it was urgent that he should do his work before the night finally closed in. As he looked at his disciples with this thought in his mind he said, however, "*We must work*". He was trying to communicate to them not only the same vision and the same deep concern as he himself had, but also the same sense of urgency.

We can assess the influence which Jesus' words had on the disciples if we turn to the book of Acts and watch them in the leadership of the early Church. They now face the same kind of world posing the same problems before which they had proved themselves so inept in their thought and so fatalistic in their attitude, but they are now transformed men. They see everything differently. Christ, crucified and risen, is now to them the light of the world, shining in a darkness that is continually in retreat. Their eyes have seen the glory of his coming, the

power of his Kingdom, and the final total surrender of everything evil to his name. They have neither time nor inclination
to indulge in any kind of analysis of the human situation or to
think out its past causes. They want to know only how and
where they must resist and attack. They are no longer on the
sidelines. They have raised their banner and they are at the
centre of the battle.

What about ourselves? We have cleared away from our
streets the beggars and the sick. The front line at which we
have to face the need of our human situation with its tragedies
and injustices has shifted. It is now on our television screens
that most of us see it. There the horror of it all presents itself to
us no less vividly than it presented itself to the early disciples in
Jerusalem, and on a much larger scale – its earthquakes,
wars, famines, brutalities, human diseases and deformities.
And still today even on the closer and more personal home
front, the same perplexing questions as plagued the disciples
can also address themselves acutely to our own minds. Why
did it all happen to us and ours? We, too, are being tested as to
how we react in mind, emotion, and will. We may not be
tempted, of course, to indulge in the same kind of Rabbinic
speculation about possible hereditary guilt as did the disciples
of Jesus, yet we ourselves can slip back sometimes into the
same fatalistic acceptance of the darkness around, out of
which Jesus tried to deliver them, and we tend at times, to add
a measure of more modern cynicism and bitterness to our
condition.

It is in this situation, above all, that we must allow Jesus'
words to convict and inspire us, to enlarge our vision and to
deliver us from all sloth and despair. We must avoid becoming
overconcerned with analysing the situation and assessing the
blame, and raising questions impossible to answer. "Our first
concern", as P.T. Forsyth once put it "is not with the riddle of
the universe, but with the tragedy of the universe." Instead of
complaining or cursing the darkness we must light our candle,
and we must recognise the shortness of the time alloted to us.
The night can come when no one can work.

The Demonstration

Jesus healed the physical blindness in an unusually elaborate way. He took clay, mixed it with his spittle, annointed the man's eyes with the mixture, and told him to go and wash in the pool of Siloam. *'He went and washed and came back seeing.'* When he had healed so many, so often, with a mere word or a simple touch, why in this case these strange additions?

Some commentators think that Jesus was here making a concession to a superstition strongly held by his patient that such a mixture of clay with the spittle of a holy man would have magical properties. We prefer however to interpret the clay and the spittle and the washing as signs deliberately given even more for the sake of the onlookers, including his own disciples, than for the sake of the man. He was giving them all a message about himself and his work.

Was this case before him not that of a man who from the beginning of his earthly life had never had eyes to see? If he were to be given sight would it not require a miracle, not simply of ordinary healing, but of the same creative power as had been exercised by God when he was originally made? Moreover, in the beginning when God made man, did he not form him from the dust of the earth and breathe into his nostrils the breath of life? Therefore Jesus took the dust of the earth, mixed it with something intimately from himself to demonstrate that he himself was in this miracle exercising the very power by which God created man at the beginning and was doing it in much the same way. The act of healing was thus "clothed in allegory", and was meant to be understood in this way by the onlookers.

The sign, of course, sets the seal on the word Jesus had spoken to his disciples. It is a clear demonstration that where he brings his influence to bear we can always expect the impossible. No situation on earth is ever so chaotic, degenerate or perverted that his touch and word today cannot transform it. Where he is active, "the old has passed away, behold, the new has come" (2 Cor. 5:17).

The Preparation for Re-birth

As we follow through the story, our attention is suddenly switched from what Jesus said to the disciples in word and sign. We now find ourselves in the midst of the quite mundane and yet fascinating details of what happened, possibly over a prolonged period, to the man who had received his physical sight. Like that of the woman at the well, it is an intimate story of the search of a soul for re-birth and renewal.

We have a key to understanding the whole incident if we notice that very soon after he begins to enjoy the marvellous social and physical freedom Jesus has now given him, one great question begins to dominate his mind: What is he to think of Jesus, and how is he to speak of him? Moreover, he has become gripped by the belief that this man Jesus, has more to give him than he has already received simply on the physical level.

With his own ears he had heard Jesus claiming to be the "light of the world" and though he has now seen the beauty of the earth and the glorious light of an ordinary day, he wants to be able to see the full radiance of that other light too. The story of his pilgrimage therefore becomes not only that of a mind searching after the truth about Jesus, but also that of a heart more and more gripped by a desire to meet him again and receive from him all his gifts in their fullness.

We can clearly trace the development in his thinking about Jesus, as he meets other people and is encouraged to talk about what has happened to himself. First of all he has to tell his former neighbours: "*The man called Jesus did it*" he says. He speaks with loving gratitude. He never forgot the kindness of that touch, and the wonderfully sympathetic words he had overheard as Jesus has spoken about him to his disciples – "*a man destined for the glory of God!*" No other body had ever made him feel that way!

The next factor in his development is his astonishment in hearing the controversy among the Pharisees when they first considered his case. Some of them tried to warn him against Jesus – a sinner who had deliberately and in public broken the Sabbath! But others of them, on hearing him, shared his own wonderment. They challenged him to give his own thoughts, and in an inspired moment he moved towards the truth: *"He is a prophet."*

Then he makes a finally decisive discovery – that where opposition to Jesus is found, it is always accompanied by a fear and hatred of him that excludes respect for his obvious truth and goodness.

The Pharisees reveal first their obstinate reluctance to face unwanted facts. They have to call his parents to prove that the miracle had really taken place. They then reveal their deviousness, suggesting to his mind that the miracle was to be attributed to a sheer unique act of God himself, and that Jesus had somehow cunningly managed to cash in on it and take the credit to himself. They continue to insist that a man that is such a sinner could not possibly have done such a thing. In a long drawn-out final conversation the man finds himself with surprising boldness entering the controversy between Jesus and his enemies decidedly on the side of Jesus, and in a moment of suddenly inspired obstinacy on his part (cf. Mk. 13:11), he affirms that Jesus must have come uniquely *"from God"* and that *"Never since the world began"* was there such a man as this!

As his thinking thus develops so his devotion and desire for Jesus himself also increase. The shock of his parents' disloyalty brought him a measure of shame, loneliness and suffering, and finally under the hatred of those whose authority he had so marvellously challenged, he finds himself cruelly excommunicated and cast out of the social life of his community.

It is at this very moment that Jesus comes to seek him out. We are meant to understand that all through his mental perplexity and searching, Jesus had been there in the background controlling his thoughts and inspiring his very seeking so that he might find (Matt. 7:7). We are meant also to understand that the intense suffering brought upon him by the desertion of his parents and the cruel final persecution had their part to play in bringing him towards the glorious light that now comes to him with the presence of Jesus. "It was in the school of affliction," it is said of Oliver Cromwell, "that he was kept till he had learned the lesson of the Cross, till his will was broken into submission to the Will of God". Religion was thus "laid into his soul with hammer and fire"; it did not "come in only as light into his understanding".

Yet it is what Jesus revealed and brought to this man quite suddenly during this final decisive encounter that made everything that had so far happened to him worthwhile. Otherwise the great miracle of his cure at the pool, his brave search for the truth and his defence of Jesus against his enemies would have been fruitless. It is as if Jesus, when he comes to this man, brings with him an open door into an entirely new world of thought and experience. His longing to believe is suddenly transformed into radiant faith. He seeks to know from Jesus alone what he must now think about Jesus himself. How futile his former thoughts have been! Could he possibly have escaped a sense of his own sinfulness as, yielding to his grace and love, *"he worshipped him"*.

This is indeed the worship "in spirit" (John 4:23) of which Jesus spoke to the woman at the well, and which he sought from her. We must not underestimate the worth of the orderly and liturgical worship "in truth" which we regularly offer to God within his Church week by week. Such observances are a reasonable service acceptable to God. Unless our liturgical worship, however, is often punctuated by such living encounters with Jesus himself (cf. Rev. 1:10 – 13) there will be unreality both in our Church services and in our confessions of our faith. The truest worship is given spontaneously from the heart when the Spirit enables us to see who it is, there before us in Jesus. This man is not yet able to express his faith and devotion in the Biblical or philosophical language that we incorporate in our great creeds or in liturgical service. But his eyes have indeed been opened to see what Peter saw when, in his fishing boat, he felt compelled to fall at Jesus' feet (Luke 5:8).

Signs of Present Judgement

Many commentators on this passage call our attention to what happened simultaneously to the Pharisees in contrast to the formerly blind man. As he has moved from interest in and gratitude to Jesus, on to inner re-birth, gradually increasing illumination, and adoring worship, so the Pharisees who have been questioning him have in the same process plunged themselves gradually into a darkness, expressed in their increasingly angry reviling, and the final act of gross cruelty towards a perfectly innocent man who had done them no harm. Jesus claimed that he himself had been instrumental in setting this process in motion. He often declared that after his Second Coming there would take place a Day of Judgement when he would bring about a final complete separation between those who were for him and those who were against him. Here he points out that much that will be revealed and sealed in this final Judgement is already taking place in history here and now.

Many of the Pharisees around Jesus then seemed to have been so blind that they were unaware of what was happening to them. Yet one or two of them took the hint that Jesus might have been referring to them. *"Are we also blind?"* they said. His reply with its urgent appeal and warning, must be allowed to come through to ourselves today, with its full original force and meaning: *"If you were blind, you would have no guilt; but now that you say, 'We see', your guilt remains."*

One of the most important discoveries Jesus wants us to make in his presence is that of our own blindness to what he has come to reveal to us – a blindness both natural and cultivated. One of the great prophets simply and profoundly describes our state before him:

'For my thoughts are not your thoughts,
neither are your ways my ways, says the Lord.
For as the heavens are higher than the earth,
so are my ways higher than your ways
and my thoughts than your thoughts.'
(Isa. 55:8 – 9)

On the most crucial matters of life and destiny we have to allow his truth to displace even the fondest ideas of our own minds, and we have to conform in our ways to the light that has shone into our darkness. Jesus described the knowledge of God and of himself as a mystery which God had "hidden . . . from the wise and understanding, and revealed . . . to babes" (Matt. 11:25). Here he refers to it as revealed to the "blind" and hidden from those who think they see.

A Note on a Parenthesis

This story was circulated in the New Testament Church with a short parenthesis referring to the Pool of Siloam, and indicating an interpretation of the washing incident which circulated with the story. We are informed, in brackets, that Siloam *"means sent"*.

Those who were spoken of as the *"Sent"* in the New Testament were the Apostles, and there was verbal similarity between *"Siloam"* and *"Sent"* in the original languages. The narrator in re-telling the story could have intended us to notice the similarity between what happened to this man through washing in Siloam, and what can happen when Christians who enter the Church are washed in Baptism which is indeed the Pool of the Apostles who were sent to preach, teach and baptize (Matt. 28:19 – 20). Baptism they believed was not only a sign of rebirth and renewal but could actually bring the same kind of illumination and enlightenment as had come to Jesus himself, and John the Baptist too, at the Jordan. The story of this man's pilgrimage from baptism towards faith and illumination, therefore, could be taken as an example of what at times could happen to those whom they themselves washed in their own special pool of baptism. Indeed, often when people were baptized in the early Church, this chapter of John's Gospel was read in the service.

Certainly it is true that often in the New Testament people were baptized after they came to faith in Jesus. Yet this order of experience was not invariable. Many of us today who were baptized in childhood will be able to recognise in this story, elements of our personal pilgrimage from Baptism to illumination and rebirth.

CHAPTER 22

THE GOOD SHEPHERD
John 10:1 – 18

10 "Truly, truly, I say to you, he who does not enter the sheepfold by the door but climbs in by another way, that man is a thief and a robber; [2]but he who enters by the door is the shepherd of the sheep. [3]To him the gatekeeper opens; the sheep hear his voice, and he calls his own sheep by name and leads them out. [4]When he has brought out all his own, he goes before them, and the sheep follow him, for they know his voice. [5]A stranger they will not follow, but they will flee from him, for they do not know the voice of strangers." [6]This figure Jesus used with them, but they did not understand what he was saying to them.

7 So Jesus again said to them, "Truly, truly, I say to you, I am the door of the sheep. [8]All who came before me are thieves and robbers; but the sheep did not heed them. [9]I am the door; if any one enters by me, he will be saved, and will go in and out and find pasture. [10]The thief comes only to steal and kill and destroy; I came that they may have life, and have it abundantly. [11]I am the good shepherd. The good shepherd lays down his life for the sheep. [12]He who is a hireling and not a shepherd, whose own the sheep are not, sees the wolf coming and leaves the sheep and flees; and the wolf snatches them and scatters them. [13]He flees because he is a hireling and cares nothing for the sheep. [14]I am the good shepherd; I know my own and my own know me, [15]as the Father knows me and I know the Father; and I lay down my life for the sheep. [16]And I have other sheep, that are not of this fold; I must bring them also, and they will heed my

voice. So there shall be one flock, one shepherd. [17]For this reason the Father loves me, because I lay down my life, that I may take it again. [18]No one takes it from me, but I lay it down of my own accord. I have power to lay it down, and I have power to take it again; this charge I have received from my Father."

An Offer of Leadership

We are told that it was at the '*feast of the Dedication at Jerusalem*' that Jesus made this claim to be "*the good shepherd*". This feast was held annually in winter to commemorate the rededication of the Temple after its cleansing and restoration under Judas Maccabaeus. During that feast there was read in the liturgy the passage in Ezekiel 34 in which God expresses his anger at those whom he calls the "shepherds" of his flock. "Shepherd" was the name he gave then to those to whom he had entrusted the political, moral and spiritual leadership of his people. But the leaders to whom he had entrusted so much had abused their power and privileges. "You clothe yourselves with the wool, you slaughter the fatlings; but you do not feed the sheep. The weak you have not strengthened, the sick you have not healed . . . my sheep were scattered over all the face of the earth, with none to search or seek for them." It is in this passage that God promises that he himself will come to be the good shepherd of Israel: "I myself will be the shepherd of my sheep, and I will make them lie down, says the Lord God. I will seek the lost . . . and I will strengthen the weak, and the fat and the strong I will watch over; I will feed them in justice."

Jesus could not resist taking up this theme as he faced the crowd around him in the Temple. That old scripture had come to life again! The false shepherds of his own day, the contemporary Jewish rulers, were all there listening to him. A day or two previously he had seen some of these very Pharisees cast out of their fellowship the man he himself had cured. Their treatment of him had been callous. He had been there in their midst blind and poor from his birth. Certainly they could not have cured his blindness, but they had not cared about his poverty. They had owed him welfare, wise guidance, encouragement in goodness and true piety. Instead, for years they had neglected him. They had not known he existed, till Jesus had himself found him. Moreover when he had come to their notice they had tried merely to bully him into mental submission and to tie him up in unhelpful discussion. Finally when he had refused to respond they had made him an outcast.

Moreover, there, facing Jesus, were many of the common people of the day. They were completely and culpably blind to the scandal in what was happening around them. Like the parents of the man he had cured they were unable even to see that in Jesus, God himself had come to be their leader, and they were meekly accepting the ruthless tyranny of those who had proved themselves more like wolves and thieves than shepherds. In what he said to his hearers, Jesus exposed the abuses that they were so meekly accepting from those above them, and he offered himself as their Good Shepherd. He had little hope. They had already rejected him when he had offered himself as the "Bread of Life" and as the "Light of the World". He already knew that soon they were going to give their final verdict on him: "We will not have this man to reign over us."

"My sheep hear my voice"

As he faced what was certain rejection by his generation Jesus knew that the very death to which they were going to subject him, would give him all the more right to lay claim to leadership not only of the Jewish nation, but of the whole human race. He therefore spoke as if he were addressing every age of mankind. We can listen to these words he spoke in the Temple courts at the feast of Dedication just as if they were addressed to us in our present circumstances. He is offering himself to us today as our leader. He is warning us, too, against the faithless leaders around us, against the powers, principles, parties and personalities, which seek within our modern world to gain from us the kind of loyalty which he who alone has died for us has the right to demand.

We cannot help hearing the repeated promise. In every age it will happen. The Good Shepherd will speak, and the sheep will follow him, for they know his voice. "*The sheep hear his voice*" (v.3). They "*follow him, for they know his voice*" (v.4). "*They will heed my voice*" (v.16). "*My sheep hear my voice, and I know them, and they follow me*" (v.27). This is the way Jesus is going to gain possession in every age of the minds and hearts of those he wants in his service. They will hear him calling, inviting, commanding, and thus they will find themselves subtly and impellingly brought under his personal influence and guidance. As they listen and respond, his word will become the dominant force in shaping their life and destiny.

The early chapters of the book of Proverbs give us a vivid picture of life as it confronted the young man in that ancient world. As he grows up and walks the streets of his world voice after voice comes to him.

His Father and Mother speak: "Hear my son, your father's instruction, and reject not your mother's teaching" (Prov. 1:8), but there are "sinners who entice", there is the thug who says, "come with us, let us lie in wait for blood" (Prov. 1:10 – 11), there is "the worthless person" who "winks with his eyes, scrapes with his feet, points with his finger", who "with perverted heart devises evil" (6:12 – 14), and there is also the harlot: "I have decked my couch with coverings, coloured spreads of Egyptian linen; I have perfumed my bed . . . Come, let us take our fill of love till morning, for my husband is not at home" (7:16 – 19). But in the background, always persistent, always seeking to save from destruction, and to control all human ways, there is one voice which he can heed if he wills, an unerring guide – the voice of Wisdom. "Doth not wisdom call, does not understanding raise her voice? On the heights beside the way, in the paths she takes her stand . . . To you O men I call, and my cry is to the sons of men" (8:1 – 4). What she says is "righteous" and "better than jewels". It enables kings to reign and "to decree what is just" (8:11,15).

Is this not a description of modern life too, as many of us grow up in it? – one voice after another, calling, advertising, tempting, offering pleasure, profit or purpose in various mixtures, to be found in new ways or old ways, in bad ways or good ways, in easy ways or hard ways? Yet in the midst of this babel of voices we can if we will, hear the voice of Jesus. It is he

who is described in the figure of wisdom in that Old
Testament passage. It is he who comes to take his stance today
to make his call heard so that those who are willing to follow
may come to know that they are his sheep, and that under his
guidance and control, human history itself has a purpose and
a meaning.

A Place and a Purpose in the Kingdom of God

Sometimes when I pass through the concourse of a great
international airport on a busy day and see masses of people of
different races, colours, backgrounds, milling here and there
with such differing business on hand and varied aims for life,
I find myself asking one or two inter-related questions. Is
there one all-embracing purpose really being worked out in
the midst of this mass of people with its great turbulent clash of
human interests? Do I as an individual have a place in that
purpose, and a personal destiny that really matters? It is the
fact that, in the midst of such a world Christ's sheep hear his
voice, that gives me a sufficient answer.

Centuries ago Abraham lived in a city that was at the centre
of international trade and travel in one of the busiest regions of
the world. Some scholars suggest that he was a transport agent
with a thriving business. Perhaps he, too, had all these
questions about himself and this thronging world to ask. But
he heard the voice of God. Abraham was told that the God of
all the earth had indeed a purpose for all nations to be worked
out through generations to come, that there was a task he
himself had to fulfil in its present working out, and a place for
himself and his children in its future glory. To know this,
changed his religion, and his way of life. Above all two of the
most important facts about life became clear to him: The God
of all the earth was working out a great purpose within its
history, and Abraham himself and his family after him, had a
place within that purpose.

God continued to fulfil the promise given to Abraham to
bring blessing to all nations. The Bible is the story of how
under changing circumstances and in varied ways he never
failed from generation to generation to call individuals and to
make the same great news known: "I have a purpose for this

world, and a place for you to fulfil in it". God called Moses at
the bush, Samuel in the sacred tent, all the great judges, kings
and prophets of Israel, John the Baptist, and the disciples in
Galilee; and now today we have the Church where he speaks
again and again with the same purpose to those who are given
ears to hear. That I hear his voice today, gives me the assurance that he is still in business, with the same plan encompass-
ing all nations, still determined finally as we move forward to
the last day to solve for us all the problems of human sin,
suffering, and destiny. When I hear his voice I know that I
myself am not lost in the crowd. I matter to him. God knows
my name. He made me what I am. He understands my history
from my birth. I begin myself to know, understand, and accept
my place in the working out of his purpose. I know that he
wants obedience from me. He wants at times to give me a new
direction. He seeks time and again to bring me back into line.
He continually empowers and liberates. His voice may not be
loud and dominant within the modern world, for when he
speaks he does not necessarily push himself into the media. It
often comes to us as the quietly spoken voice in the
background of life. We remember how once Elijah heard it. It
came in a "still small voice" after the earthquake, wind and
fire had proved with all their spectacular fury that they had
nothing of any importance to convey. A foreman on a factory
floor can lift up a telephone and in the midst of the continuous
clash and din of machinery with men shouting at each other
across the floor, can put his ear close to the receiver and hear
the voice that matters with the message that matters.

The Credentials of the True Shepherd

We have to take note at this point of how Jesus dealt directly
with his contemporary situation. In a series of vivid pictures
and comparisons he brings out the contrast between himself
and the false leaders of his own day, especially the Pharisees,
underlining at the same time some unique features of his own
leadership. As we follow this theme we find, as we have
already pointed out, that his purpose widens. We find him
giving us the pattern which he wished to be followed by those
who had responsibility for leadership in the service of his own

Church and Kingdom. We find also that his teaching has something to say to us about the leadership we cultivate within the secular world today.

Jesus first of all contrasts the approach of those he calls *"thieves and robbers"*, who come to steal our support and loyalty by their own cunning, with the frank approach of him who has a genuine cause. In making this comparison, he takes us immediately to the heart of modern life. Often, because the ideas and aims of a movement do not stand up under searching examination, its leaders and sponsors as they seek to win adherents resort to subterfuge. Only the best few cards are put on the table. Only partial aspects of the programme are presented, and great emphasis is laid on the need for the creation of a "public image" often different from the reality, by advertising and effective media coverage, to disarm suspicion and lull the critical facilities. Jesus aptly describes the furtiveness and stealth of such an approach, as he warns us to beware of the leader *"who does not enter the sheepfold by the door, but climbs in by another way"*.

Jesus describes his own approach. The shepherd who is worthy of trust is *"he who enters by the door"*. Openness – Glasnost! Nothing is hidden from the start. There is no "small print". He himself is transparent, and his teaching is like himself. He makes no attempt to woo people with attractive promises and free gifts, before the difficulties and demands are made clear. From the very beginning we know that there is sin to be faced, guilt to be settled, a cross to be taken up daily, and a self to be denied as well as glorious liberty, a place within the family of God, and a heaven, to be gained.

Jesus contrasts the kind of relationship that is set up through his manner of open approach, with that created by the leader who takes another way. The *"thieves and robbers"* may indeed gain some kind of admittance and achieve some kind of following by their stealth. But there can never be anything truly deep or finally effective in the movement they create, or its achievements. The openness and trustworthiness of the good shepherd, however, creates true openness, trust and loyalty in his sheep. As he makes his approach, *"to him the gatekeeper opens; the sheep hear his voice, and he calls his own sheep by name and leads them out ... and the sheep follow him, for they know his voice"*.

Moreover, Jesus observes, as his followers respond to him, one of the first things they learn is the ability to distinguish the genuine from the sham. They learn to shun the superficial and the twisted. Jesus therefore pictures what will happen when anyone with any deep insincerity makes his approach: "*A stranger they will not follow, but they will flee from him, for they do not know the voice of strangers.*"

This description by Jesus of his own approach to his future mission and of the people he is aiming to gather under his leadership, gives us cause for reflection, and examination of our own presentation of the faith, and our aim in building up his Church. Sometimes because we are not entirely sure of the convincing power of a completely clear and direct approach to people with the unabridged truth itself, are we not apt to lay too much emphasis on the technique of impressive presentation? Do we not overvalue what we think is the effectiveness of "personality" and "charisma"? Do we not tend, moreover, to select those aspects of Jesus and his teaching which we imagine to be especially attractive to our hearers, and to hide what we think might put people off, thus adding a touch of deceit to our whole approach? Perhaps some do not respond to us wholeheartedly because they feel almost unconsciously that we are not entirely true to either Jesus, or to life as it really is. Paul shows us more clearly the way appealed for by Jesus: "We have renounced disgraceful, underhand ways: we refuse to practice cunning or to tamper with God's word, but by the open statement of the truth, we would commend ourselves to every man's conscience in the sight of God" (2 Cor. 4:2).

We find that with the mention of the word "*stranger*" and his description of his own intimacy with his sheep, Jesus had led our thoughts into another contrast – that between the distance which often prevails in the world between the leader and the led, and the intimate closeness with himself, into which he seeks to draw those who follow him. There is no doubt that in certain spheres of the world's life effective leadership and authority is maintained often by artificial means, and sometimes by a superficial show of dignity. In the armed forces and justiciary uniforms with insignia, and "robes" of office are worn. In bureaucracy and business, authority is sometimes maintained by an official manner behind an office desk. Rules, ceremonies and etiquette become barriers to real closeness. The distance is sacrosanct. Yet, Jesus himself is satisfied with nothing less than the warm intimacy that inspires love and a much greater loyalty "*I know my own and my own know me*". The good shepherd must call "*his own sheep by name*".

Other characteristics of Jesus' pastoral leadership come to mind as we read through his words about himself. His intimacy with us of course involves humility. Moreover, he is always available. No need to make appointments, or to observe office hours with this kind of leader – take up the 'phone anytime!

As he brings his discourse to an end, he takes us to the heart of his own ministry as he warns us of the dangers against which the sheep have no defence unless the leader is watchful and utterly loyal. He envisages such danger everywhere in the form of the false leader, the thief who "*comes only to steal and kill and destroy*", and in the form of the wolf; the threat of whose coming is so terrible that he scares away every type of leader, except the one who is prepared "*to lay down his life for the sheep*". It would be justifiable to imagine the "*thief*" here to be the teacher of false doctrine (always a danger as he intrudes in the Church) and the "*wolf*" to be the anti-Christian persecutor of those who profess loyalty to the Gospel. Rather than give encouragement to such detailed speculation, Jesus is more concerned here to bring before us his own personal example of true watchfulness and loyalty. Recalling his experience of Palestine in former days, George Adam Smith writes: "I do not remember ever to have seen in the East a flock of sheep without a shepherd . . . on some high moor – across which at night the hyenas howl – when you meet him sleepless, far-sighted, weather-beaten, armed, leaning on his staff and looking out over his scattered sheep, everyone of them on his heart, you understand . . . why Christ took him as the type of self-sacrifice."

It is the danger that we might become "hirelings" that occupies Jesus' mind as he draws his discourse to an end. Under the trials and dangers involved in his service, the hireling "*flees because he is a hireling and cares nothing for the sheep*". It is our inward attitude of mind that is here in question. Most of us who have taken on the responsibility of leadership within our community are of course hired teachers, probation officers, doctors, nurses, welfare workers and pastors too. There is nothing wrong in this. "The labourer is worthy of his hire" (Luke 10:7). What matters especially in the ministry of the Church is that we should never come under the suspicion of being a "hireling" – calculating, bargaining, demanding, setting limits, expecting exemplary response from the sheep, and giving way to slackness or depression when our expectations are not met. The motto of the greatest of the Apostles is in place here: "I will most gladly spend and be spent for your souls" (2 Cor. 12:15).

One Flock : One Shepherd

Towards the end of the discourse Jesus gives us one important direct glimpse into a future development which he wished to see in his Church. "*I have other sheep, that are not of this fold; I must bring them also, and they will heed my voice. So there shall be one flock, one shepherd.*" When he was speaking, of course, Israel was "*this fold*" from which he was seeking to gather his own sheep. Even in the midst of this task, however, he speaks of those "*other sheep*" which he will gather from elsewhere – from all nations. Here is the vision, which he communicated to the Apostles, of the world mission of the Church – one flock and one shepherd.

This single text is not the best place from which to make comments on his desire for unity in his Church, or on the larger Church structure which can best express this unity. The whole passage before us, however, does suggest that Jesus envisaged everywhere the development of local Churches, each under the ministry of its own "*one shepherd*", who would reflect in his care for his flock the characteristics of leadership which have been so carefully described here in his discourse.

In the fulfilment of this ministry one of the chief tasks of the local Pastor is to preach so that his people can hear the voice of the Good Shepherd himself. There is no doubt that the Word of God will often have to be delivered and heard through his ministry in much the same way as many of the oracles of the prophets were delivered and heard by their contemporaries.

Preaching, according to the New Testament, is often the public proclamation of the Good News of the Gospel, to whomever will hear, by the herald and messenger of God. Peter's great sermon on the day of Pentecost, and many other sermons in the book of Acts, were stirring public addresses, and Jesus himself preached at times in this way to great multitudes. Preaching even by the local Pastor to his congregation can be a very "public" affair.

Yet many of us who have found ourselves called to minister to a local congregation will find in this present chapter further important insights into our task as preacher. All the Gospels show that, though Jesus loved to address the crowds around him, he loved it almost better to speak when he was face to face with a solitary individual talking about deeply individual matters. It was often through this kind of conversation that he won personal trust, and forgave people their sins. He spoke of how he loved to seek out the one among the many (cf. Luke 15:7,10) and once, when a huge crowd of people was thronging round him, he showed how sensitive he himself was to the mere touch of one poor woman who was desperately seeking his help (Mark 5:31). "Many thronged him", said Augustine of this occasion, "one touched him". It has been observed that Jesus' "best sermons" were sometimes preached to one person.

When a Pastor becomes fully aware that Jesus seeks, through his ministry in the pulpit, to enter this kind of private and personal conversation with those who are listening to him, it can affect the manner and style of his speaking, and the structure of his ministry. Even though there may be a comparatively "large" congregation in front of him, he will tend not to be satisfied simply with addressing people *en masse* in the hope that somehow some relevant word may be overheard here and there. He will, rather, be concerned to express his message as a word personally, and at times quietly and intimately, directed to a particular individual. He may tend to feel that a low-key conversational approach to his hearers is best fitted to his task. He himself will discover a way of putting things so that he can often himself address the individual at the same time as he is also speaking to the crowd.

It is, moreover, both fitting and inevitable that the Pastor who finds himself engaged in such a ministry in the pulpit will seek to follow it up by himself seeking entrance, as far as is humanly possible, into the same kind of personal relationship with each member of his flock, as Christ himself is seeking. He cannot allow himself to remain in any way remote from his people – a *"stranger"* whom the sheep *"will not follow"*. Because he has accepted the call to be their shepherd, then by this capacity he belongs to them, and they to him. He will not be able to regard his ministry in the pulpit as sound, unless, as a continuation of it he seeks out his people where they are to be found with their questions and needs, both in the routine and especially in the sufferings of their ordinary lives. His visitation of the flock, even though it may sometimes appear to be the fulfilment of a routine duty, can become a symbol of the continuing care and concern of Christ for each and all. Indeed at special times it can become a sign, that the Good Shepherd himself has *"laid down his life for the sheep"*.

We must not in any way undervalue the tradition, which, inspired by this chapter of John's Gospel, has persisted throughout Church history, within every Christian denomination, of the local pastor who gives his life to the ministry of the Word and Sacraments, and to pastoral visitation. Paul at Ephesus first gave the example and laid down the standard in his sermon to the Pastors at Ephesus when he spoke of how for three years "I did not cease night or day to admonish everyone with tears", teaching "in public and from house to house", and pled with them. "Take heed to yourselves and to all the flock, in which the Holy Spirit has made you guardians, to feed the Church of the Lord which he obtained with his own blood" (Acts 20:20, 28, 31).

Of course within the Church each member of the body is called to serve others, and the whole body in the name of Christ. A rich variety of differing ministries represents various aspects of the one ministry of Christ to the Church. It is, however, through what the local Pastor is called to do that the ministry of Christ, the Good Shepherd, is most fully represented and can be made most fully effective. Calvin went to the length of saying of the Pastor that he was the one whom above all Christ has appointed to "represent his own person", and the "chief sinew by which believers are held together in one body". We have to ask ourselves whether the size of many modern congregations does not prevent the "Pastor" who preaches from himself reflecting fully enough the picture given here by Jesus, and whether even a team of other pastors under him can really make up for the defects both in the image and in the preaching.

The Appeal to enter the "Door"

Many of Jesus' parables encourage us to think of his Kingdom as an influence that can enter us here and now when we hear and receive the Word of God. It is like seed sown within us. It grows within us, affecting the life of the world around us, and thus human history. At the final great consummation at the end of history everything that has been achieved through its influence will be harvested for God's eternal glory and use. There are other parables, however, that encourage us to think of the Kingdom of God not only as if it were a powerful inner influence on personal and social life, but as if it were a new world already existing alongside this world. Jesus likens it to another realm, the door into which is open here and now to all whom he invites in. To enter offers joyful fellowship, enlargement of life and blessedness. He spoke in this way when he described the Kingdom as a Wedding Feast (Matt. 22:1 – 10) or as a Great Supper into which the needy and deprived were to be even compelled to enter in order to enjoy what was lavishly prepared and freely given. There was no need to wait. "Come, for all is now ready" (Luke 14:16).

Jesus is further encouraging us in this latter kind of thought about the Kingdom when he says of himself "*I am the door*". In our personal encounter with him as he comes to us in the midst of this world's life there is opened to us a way of entry, an access, into that New World of which he spoke in these parables. The suggestion is that we should think of ourselves, even while living within this present world, as always on the border of another. Jesus himself, who invites us in to that other world, also leads us across and back over the border between the two. He "*calls his own sheep by name and leads them out.*" He also "*goes before them*" when he has "*brought out all his own*". We ourselves thus go " *'in and out*" by him. Jesus here describes himself as especially at home within that other world to which he is the "*door*". At times he calls us in there to himself to find pasture, only then to lead us back, refreshed, to our life on earth under his guidance.

Such thoughts of our life with Christ as lived between two realms became more explicit in the minds of the Apostles, and were given a prominent part in their message. When they saw Jesus lifted up from the earth and disappearing they thought of him as having gone back to the realm from which he had come. They believed that he had opened a way for them to have fellowship with him in heaven. But they experienced also the coming of the Spirit, and they knew that he was also here and now, with them on earth guiding and helping them always "even to the close of the age". When they spoke of their experience of him, therefore, they spoke not only of his presence with them on earth, but also of their having been "translated" to be in some way and measure, with him in heaven. There they had their "citizenship" and their hidden life. They were already "raised up with him" and made to sit in "heavenly places" (Phil. 3:20; Col. 3:3; Eph. 2:6). They had already indeed had a foretaste or "guarantee" of things to come, of the full inheritance which would finally be given to them when this present world had passed away (Eph. 1:14, Rom. 8:23).

We will perhaps understand best the thrust of Jesus' words about his being the "door" if we look on them as a sudden and spontaneous evangelistic appeal prompted by some whom he spotted among his hearers. Might it not be that he saw Nicodemus there listening to him? – and there may also have been others whom he had challenged already to seek birth from above into the Kingdom of God. Some scholars think that we have in this discourse the account of two very different parables spoken on different occasions and now brought together. There is no need for such a hypothesis. Jesus is not here switching his thought from one theme to another. He continues throughout to describe himself as the Shepherd. At the end of this discourse he offers himself as the Shepherd who will lead his sheep finally through death when it comes. Here in our present verses he is the Shepherd who here and now, without delay, can lead us into that other realm, the Kingdom of which he so often speaks.

Accepting his leadership in orienting ourselves towards the world to come, Jesus promises that we *"will be saved"*. He regarded it as tragic indeed that any of us should live with our treasure and our reward only in what is found in this present world (Matt. 6:19 – 20, Luke 12:16 – 21).

He promises, too, that we *"will go in and out and find pasture"*. These phrases suggest an offer of liberty, satisfaction and enlargement of experience such as those who live in this one world alone can never attain. As the hymn writer put it: "Solid joys and lasting pleasures, none but Zion's children know". One of the important factors in bringing about the conversion of John Bunyan was his hearing "godly talk" by a few older women. "They spoke as if joy did make them speak", and there was "such an appearance of grace" in all that they said, that they seemed to have found a new world to which he was altogether a stranger. Bunyan was humbled, and drawn again and again into their company, before he himself found the door.

CHAPTER 23

THE HARDENING OF THE RELUCTANT
John 10:19 – 42

19 There was again a division among the Jews because of these words. [20]Many of them said, "He has a demon, and he is mad; why listen to him?" [21]Others said, "These are not the sayings of one who has a demon. Can a demon open the eyes of the blind?"

22 It was the feast of the Dedication at Jerusalem; [23]it was winter, and Jesus was walking in the temple, in the portico of Solomon. [24]So the Jews gathered round him and said to him, "How long will you keep us in suspense? If you are the Christ, tell us plainly." [25]Jesus answered them, "I told you, and you do not believe. The works that I do in my Father's name, they bear witness to me; [26]but you do not believe, because you do not belong to my sheep. [27]My sheep hear my voice, and I know them, and they follow me; [28]and I give them eternal life, and they shall never perish, and no one shall snatch them out of my hand. [29]My Father, who has given them to me, is greater than all, and no one is able to snatch them out of the Father's hand. [30] I and the Father are one."

31 The Jews took up stones again to stone him. [32]Jesus answered them, "I have shown you many good works from the Father; for which of these do you stone me?" [33]The Jews answered him, "We stone you for no good work but for blasphemy; because you, being a man, make yourself God." [34]Jesus answered them, "Is it not written in your law, 'I said, you are gods'? [35]If he called them gods to whom the word of God came (and scripture cannot be broken), [36]do you say of him whom the Father consecrated and sent into the world, 'You are

blaspheming,' because I said, 'I am the Son of God'?
[37]If I am not doing the works of my Father, then do not
believe me; [38]but if I do them, even though you do not
believe me, believe the works, that you may know and
understand that the Father is in me and I am in the
Father." [39]Again they tried to arrest him, but he
escaped from their hands.

40 He went away again across the Jordan to the place
where John at first baptized, and there he remained.
[41]And many came to him; and they said, "John did no
sign, but everything that John said about this man was
true." [42]And many believed in him there.

If Jesus was to be crucified there had to be a hard enough core
of important people determined to take whatever risk might
be involved in order to carry the whole affair to the end. We
have already seen how during the controversy in the Temple
at the feast of Tabernacles, one partly sympathetic section of
the crowd became wholly alienated from him as, listening to
him more carefully than before, they took offence at his claim
to be uniquely related to God. This section of the narrative
tells how another significant minority among the "Jews", at
first uncertain and hesitant to condemn him, finally threw in
their lot with the majority.

After they had listened to his discourse on the Good
Shepherd they were finding it difficult to resist the strength of
his appeal to what was still left of honesty in their make-up,
and they may have been unhappy about the irrationality and
bitterness their leadership was showing in the affair. They
found it impossible to take seriously the accusation that "*He
has a demon*" – "*Can a demon open the eyes of the blind?*" Yet they
found aspects of his teaching disturbing and they were not able
to define the reason.

They formed themselves as a group apart from those who
had already made up their minds, and, they went to Jesus
hoping he would say something that would help them come to
an independent decision. They stated clearly what they felt
they had against him, "*How long will you keep us in suspense? If
you are the Christ, tell us plainly*". Listening to him they had
become confused. Sometimes they had been thrilled with

what he had said. At other times he said things they did not
expect their kind of Christ to claim.

It must have taken Jesus by surprise to be accused of lack of
clarity – the very fault he had always shunned, and for which
he had so severely blamed the false teachers of his day. He
immediately pointed out that the confusion lay entirely within
their own minds. *"You do not believe, because you do not belong to my
sheep."* Since the fault lay in themselves, the cure also lay in
themselves. They must now allow his clear light to cast out the
darkness of their own minds and in this way decide to belong
to him. His word brings before us again the challenge we have
heard at least twice before in this Gospel; the challenge to an
obedience prior to understanding, to a response with our wills
and minds so that we may have freedom from suspense and
doubt (John 7:17, 8:31 – 2).

At the same time he gave them another chance to come to
the very decision they had so far evaded. The point at which
we are most likely to win people over to the faith is often the
point which on first encounter tends to offend them. Jesus
therefore had to challenge them again with some of the very
words that had already attracted and yet troubled them, and
involved them in controversy with their fellow Jews. He again
made it clear that if they were to become his disciples they
must indeed become like sheep before him, ready to be led,
with minds open to his own personal influence; *"My sheep hear
my voice, and I know them, and they follow me."*

Having made his challenge and demands perfectly clear he
added no less clear words of promise and assurance: *"and I give
them eternal life, and they shall never perish, and no one shall snatch
them out of my hand."* Of course knowing his custom we expect
the word that followed. He nearly always spoke about the
Father when he spoke about his own place in the eternal
world: *"My Father, who has given them to me"*, he said, *"is greater
than all, and no one is able to snatch them out of the Father's hand. I and
the Father are one."*

Did ever the light of truth and heaven shine as clearly into
the darkness of the human mind as it did to those men who first
heard these words from Jesus? Through the centuries often
they have become the chief source of comfort, assurance and
strength to doubting and sincere souls, sometimes at the point

of despair, sometimes at death. Yet at the time they were spoken, those whom they were aimed to win to himself heard only what shocked them: "*You, being a man, make yourself God*", they said, and they "*took up stones again to stone him*". It is to be noted that they took up the stones before they began any further discussion with him.

Jesus began his defence with a simple appeal to them to become reasonable, and to see how foolish and unjust the inner hatred, that was now discovering itself, was making them. "*I have shown you many good works from the Father; for which of these do you stone me?*" It was the same kind of self-defence with which, when struck by the officer of the high priest, he made his reply: "If I have spoken wrongly, bear witness to the wrong, but if I have spoken rightly, why do you strike me?" (John 18:23).

It is perhaps significant that they did not attempt to answer him. The question therefore still remains open and unanswered today in the midst of so much reactionary, confused and often irrational criticism by so many, of what traditional Christianity has done for us. It comes as a challenge to probe our motives and the facts of the case: "honestly, does anything I have done justify the stones you have in your hand?"

The argument from Scripture with which Jesus followed this protest is bound to seem strange to us. A Psalmist in one place had even used the term "gods" to describe earthly rulers. Why then should they raise such strong objection to the language Jesus had used? It was the kind of argument they used with each other in their own theological discussion, and Jesus knew they were at home with it.

We are now told about the place of retreat in which Jesus had been able to find safety, and indeed a place to work in, during the days in which he had to wait till he knew he had to appear again in Jerusalem to bring everything to a head. It was "*across the Jordan where John at first baptized*". The Baptist's influence was there still powerful and lasting. It is at this point that we hear the last and perhaps the finest testimony to his ministry: "*John did no sign, but everything that John said about this man was true.*"

CHAPTER 24

THE RAISING OF LAZARUS – I

John 11:1 – 16

11 Now a certain man was ill, Lazarus of Bethany, the village of Mary and her sister Martha. ²It was Mary who anointed the Lord with ointment and wiped his feet with her hair, whose brother Lazarus was ill. ³So the sisters sent to him, saying, "Lord, he whom you love is ill." ⁴But when Jesus heard it he said, "This illness is not unto death; it is for the glory of God, so that the Son of God may be glorified by means of it."

5 Now Jesus loved Martha and her sister and Lazarus. ⁶So when he heard that he was ill, he stayed two days longer in the place where he was. ⁷Then after this he said to the disciples, "Let us go into Judaea again." ⁸The disciples said to him, "Rabbi, the Jews were but now seeking to stone you, and are you going there again?" ⁹Jesus answered, "Are there not twelve hours in the day? If any one walks in the day, he does not stumble, because he sees the light of this world. ¹⁰But if any one walks in the night, he stumbles, because the light is not in him." ¹¹Thus he spoke, and then he said to them, "Our friend Lazarus has fallen asleep, but I go to awake him out of sleep." ¹²The disciples said to him, "Lord, if he has fallen asleep, he will recover." ¹³Now Jesus had spoken of his death, but they thought that he meant taking rest in sleep. ¹⁴Then Jesus told them plainly, "Lazarus is dead; ¹⁵and for your sake I am glad that I was not there, so that you may believe. But let us go to him." ¹⁶Thomas, called the Twin, said to his fellow disciples, "Let us also go, that we may die with him."

Our Human Intimacies and Eternal Life

"I am sure, "wrote Paul, "that neither death, nor life, nor angels, nor principalities, nor things present, nor things to come, nor powers, nor height, nor depth, nor anything else in all creation, will be able to separate us from the love of God in Christ Jesus our Lord" (Rom. 8:38). We often read this verse at funerals, because it gives us all the assurance we need that there is a life after death for each individual with whom God has been able to establish a warm and close relationship. He will not allow death to deprive him of such a friend. Jesus himself as we have seen, expressed the same kind of argument for life after death when having described the close earthly relationship between his sheep and himself he said, "I give them eternal life, and they shall never perish" (10:28).

After having heard Jesus state so clearly in the tenth chapter of John that not even death can separate him from his friends, we find him in the eleventh chapter acting out in real life exactly what he has said. A crucial challenge, and a divinely planned opportunity came to him to do so. Lazarus, a very special friend of his, has taken ill. His sisters sent him an urgent message, hoping he would hurry to their home to cure him before he died. But he was so far away that by the time the message reached him Lazarus was dead. Jesus knew it, yet he felt immediately challenged by the message, and recognized his opportunity. He had already spoken of the hour "when the dead will hear the voice of the Son of God, and those who hear will live" (5:25). He was now in a position to give a sign − and it would probably be his last and greatest sign! − of how his friend Lazarus, even buried in his grave for days, yet not separated from him, could hear his voice and come forth to life.

This particular sign, brings to us more than the mere assurance of our individual survival after death. It enables us to see beyond this life into something of the next. We sometimes ask what is it like − that life after death? The New Testament in its answer, in order to comfort us, sometimes resorts simply to negatives: "death shall be no more, neither shall there be mourning nor crying nor pain" (Rev. 21:4; cf. 21:23,27; 22:3 − 5). Here in this chapter however, we are given a more positive and revealing hint about it: *"now Jesus loved Martha and her sister and Lazarus."* This simple statement would be superfluous here, were it not meant by the writer to convey infinite meaning.

Is it not the case that very often the most precious characteristics that mark us out in human life as distinctive individuals are given their fullest expression, and can be appreciated most, within the closest ties which God enables us to form with each other, sometimes within the life of a family, sometimes within ordinary friendship? Indeed what is of most value in our human nature can often unfold and develop best within such close relationships. Jesus found that within this closely bound family at Bethany he was in a circle of intimacy in the midst of which he loved to be. Of course he had a distinctive place for each in his heart, but he valued them more fully and appreciated them best as he watched and enjoyed them together.

Jesus therefore made his journey that day to Bethany not only because he wanted to raise Lazarus but also because he wanted to restore what Martha and Mary and Lazarus together had given him. He hated even the thought of the break up by death of those tender and true relationships in which his personal human life too had found enrichment. The special mention here of this intention as being in his mind and heart surely encourages us to hope and believe that he has the same love today for what people are in their togetherness, and the same concern to restore in the life to come the precious relationships and friendships which have come to be, because he has led and guided and enriched the human life into which he has found entrance.

Jesus cared about family life. His teaching, of course, shows how closely he was involved in every detail of it, in all its tensions, anxieties, sorrows and joys. It may be a significant feature of John's Gospel that both the first and the last of the miracles we are shown, reveal his concern for the family. They tell us that we need him amongst us continually, both when we are in the midst of our happy home celebrations, and also our deepest family sorrows. They reveal that he hated everything that can destroy its health or break it up, and that he is willing to be in the midst whether it be in joy or sorrow to give his saving help.

An Illness – for the Glory of God

The request to go to Bethany meant much more to Jesus than simply a call from friends for help, and an opportunity to stage the most remarkable sign of his whole career.

For weeks he had been waiting for a sign from his Father that the time had come for him to challenge his enemies in the Jewish community to do their worst, fulfil their plans and put him to death. The Gospel story makes it clear that that exact day could not be decided by the Jews. They would have had it all over by now if it had been in their power to do so. Jesus, up till now, had felt that the time had not yet come, and had himself been hesitant. While he had continued to provoke the anger of his enemies, he had often withdrawn himself when the tension was mounting dangerously, and at this particular period had deliberately retreated to a safe distance. He had been waiting for the Father to decide and to let him know. Complete clarity about the way ahead came to him, however, immediately the message from the sisters arrived. He knew that the time had come, and that what had happened to Lazarus was God's way of setting in motion the whole final chain of events that was to bring salvation to the world he had now learned to love so much: "*This illness*" he said, "*is not unto death; it is for the glory of God, so that the Son of God may be glorified by means of it.*"

St John's Gospel, in its story of the last days of Jesus, makes it clear that the raising of Lazarus, witnessed by a large gathering of people, was a decisive factor in forcing the hand of the "Jews". They were suddenly afraid of the possibility that he might again become popular, and were forced into desperate and speedy action. Indeed because the raised Lazarus was such a convincing proof of Jesus' power, they now planned to put him to death (11:45, 12:9 – 10).

When Jesus realised how significant for himself and his purposes the hour was, "*he stayed two days longer in the place where he was*". Possibly he wanted to ensure that death would have such a firm hold over Lazarus that he could demonstrate all the more triumphantly that he had come indeed to release his people from its power.

Other reasons for the delay also come to our mind. He may

have felt that at such a momentous turn of events he needed
time to think things out, to collect himself and pray and plan.
Though inwardly in sacrificial tension, it has to be made clear
that he makes his way towards the Cross with sovereign
majesty. He is himself master of the whole situation. It was not
fitting that he should appear now to be under compulsion or in
haste. "I lay down my life that I may take it again. No one
takes it from me, but I lay it down of my own accord" (10:18).

Twelve Hours in a Day

The writer of the narrative brings out the contrast between the
majestic courage and calmness of Jesus and the fear that
tended to invade the minds of his disciples. It had been
haunting them occasionally since the time they finally left
Galilee to go towards Jerusalem. On that journey at one
juncture as he was walking ahead to them, "they were amazed
and those who followed were afraid" (Mark 10:32). Now they
expressed their fear also on his account: *"Rabbi, the Jews were
but now seeking to stone you, and are you going there again?"* Thomas
had to rally them in their hesitancy: *"Let us also go, that we may
die with him."*

Jesus at this moment expressed his mind and revealed the
secret of his own majesty and peace in a word with which he
tried both to encourage and warn them. It comes to us as one
of these sayings with which his followers in every age are
meant to live: *"Are there not twelve hours in the day? If any one walks
in the day, he does not stumble because he sees the light of this world. But
if any one walks in the night, he stumbles, because the light is not in
him."*

Those who read and ponder the Old Testament will
understand some of the thoughts that were on Jesus' mind as
he faced this last phase of his life on earth. Waiting for his
"time" to come he may have had thoughts about the third
Chapter of Ecclesiastes: "there is . . . a time for every matter
under heaven . . . a time for war, and a time for peace"
(Eccles. 3:1 and 8). At the same time his mind may have
been dwelling on the utterance of the Psalmist in the kind
of Psalm which occupied his mind during his hours on the
Cross.

> "But I trust in thee, O Lord,
> I say, 'Thou art my God'.
> My times are in thy hand;
> Deliver me from the hand of my enemies"
> (Ps. 31:14 – 15).

Undoubtedly before he spoke to his disciples he had in mind one of these eloquent and penetrating warnings uttered by Jeremiah to Israel.

> "Give glory to the Lord your God
> before he brings darkness,
> before your feet stumble
> on the twilight mountains,
> and while you look for light
> he turns it into gloom
> and makes it deep darkness"
> (Jer. 13:16).

He himself was taking this warning to heart: Only if we live giving glory to God in perfect obedience can we walk in the daylight granted to us by God. Any attempt to evade that way involves us in the darkness and the danger in which we will inevitably become lost.

We can understand from such inner thoughts the meaning of his own unforgettable word: Each of us on our way has an exactly appointed day of life before us – a full twelve hours. It might be a short day, or it might be a long day but it is a full day. To live in the light of Christ and for the glory of God, is to walk in the day and that day will have its full twelve hours. Only for one reason can tragedy come to us – that in our folly we should seek to evade the night or prolong day. Then, indeed, we *are* in the night and we stumble. I have a note of a simple and practical interpretation of this text which I took years ago from somebody else's sermon: Duty is above everything, and duty, whether life be long or short, can make it full. And if it be full even though it has been but a breath on a glass, it has had its twelve hours. The pathos of life lies not in its shortness but in its misuse, long or short. For it is not quantity that counts but quality.

On the BBC overseas service I once heard an interview with

a woman who had been told that she had only two or three weeks to live. She was about forty, and she had three teenage children, and had always been a committed Christian. She was being interviewed by her local pastor with his tape-recorder. She began by saying how glad she was that her doctor had respected her enough to tell her the truth. She was asked if her values had changed now – and what did she regret most about the past. "I wish I had played a little more with the children, and prayed more," she said. "And what kind of thing do you want to do now?" she was asked. "Well," she replied, "just to go on doing what has to be done: living, loving, rejoicing."

CHAPTER 25

THE RAISING OF LAZARUS – II
John 11:17 – 44

17 Now when Jesus came, he found that Lazarus had already been in the tomb four days. [18]Bethany was near Jerusalem, about two miles off, [19]and many of the Jews had come to Martha and Mary to console them concerning their brother. [20]When Martha heard that Jesus was coming, she went and met him, while Mary sat in the house. [21]Martha said to Jesus, "Lord, if you had been here, my brother would not have died. [22]And even now I know that whatever you ask from God, God will give you." [23]Jesus said to her, "Your brother will rise again." [24]Martha said to him, "I know that he will rise again in the resurrection at the last day." [25]Jesus said to her, "I am the resurrection and the life; he who believes in me, though he die, yet shall he live, [26]and whoever lives and believes in me shall never die. Do you believe this?" [27]She said to him, "Yes, Lord; I believe that you are the Christ, the Son of God, he who is coming into the world."

28 When she had said this, she went and called her sister Mary, saying quietly, "The Teacher is here and is calling for you." [29]And when she heard it, she rose quickly and went to him. [30]Now Jesus had not yet come to the village, but was still in the place where Martha had met him. [31]When the Jews who were with her in the house, consoling her, saw Mary rise quickly and go out, they followed her, supposing that she was going to the tomb to weep there. [32]Then Mary, when she came where Jesus was and saw him, fell at his feet, saying to him, "Lord, if you had been here, my brother would not have died." [33]When Jesus saw her weeping, and the

206

Jews who came with her also weeping, he was deeply moved in spirit and troubled; [34]and he said, "Where have you laid him?" They said to him, "Lord, come and see." [35]Jesus wept. [36]So the Jews said, "See how he loved him!" [37]But some of them said, "Could not he who opened the eyes of the blind man have kept this man from dying?"

38 Then Jesus, deeply moved again, came to the tomb; it was a cave, and a stone lay upon it. [39]Jesus said, "Take away the stone." Martha, the sister of the dead man, said to him, "Lord, by this time there will be an odour, for he has been dead four days." [40]Jesus said to her, "Did I not tell you that if you would believe you would see the glory of God?" [41]So they took away the stone. And Jesus lifted up his eyes and said, "Father, I thank thee that thou hast heard me. [42]I knew that thou hearest me always, but I have said this on account of the people standing by, that they may believe that thou didst send me." [43]When he had said this, he cried with a loud voice, "Lazarus, come out." [44]The dead man came out, his hands and feet bound with bandages, and his face wrapped with a cloth. Jesus said to them, "Unbind him, and let him go."

Bethany and Jerusalem

Bethany, we are told, was about *"two miles off"* from Jerusalem. It was far enough away to have a distinct community life of its own. It was no doubt one of the deliberate purposes of the evangelist to give us this pleasant glimpse of social life in Bethany in order to show us that life around the city could go on here and there with sanity and sweetness even at the same time as the atmosphere at the centre of things was growing heavy with gross corruption and hatred of God, and was thus becoming void of goodness. The writer of this Gospel was not an anti-Semitist. He wants us to know that *many of the Jews*, the local friends of Mary and Martha, were normal, kindly and good people. When Lazarus died they all rallied round their bereaved friends, shared with them their faith in the final resurrection of the dead, and brought them the comfort of their presence. They helped and encouraged them to weep, for this was the best therapy treatment they could give to each other in those days.

As the story proceeds, however, we are soon sharply to be reminded again of the contrast between these "Jews" and those within the city who were consumed by hatred of Jesus. This is an ominous note here in the mention that Bethany (though two miles off!) was yet "*near Jerusalem*". It was too near! What was so tender and human in Bethany was all too soon and too easily to become infected and destroyed by the powers that be in Jerusalem. It was the usual tragic story of what happens to goodness and truth when a people allow themselves to be taken over by evil leaders and powers. It tormented a prophet like Jeremiah to see such a situation in his day, and to know so certainly that corruption and godlessness had taken such a strong grip of the social and religious life of his people that what still remained in the midst of true worth, and simple human goodness, had inevitably to become crushed in the judgement he himself had finally to pronounce in the name of God upon the whole nation.

Jesus, Martha and Mary

When Jesus arrived he found that Martha and Mary were both troubled especially about the way it had all happened to themselves and Lazarus. Up to the end of his illness they had been praying fervently, watching and hoping that the Master would come before their brother died. They had all the more difficulty in accepting what happened because their hope had been so strong. They were reproaching themselves for not realising sooner how critical the illness really was, and for not sending the message earlier. And why had Jesus himself taken so long in arriving? Both of them unburdened their hearts and minds to him with the same words "*Lord, if you had been here, my brother would not have died*".

How human they were! So often after every kind of tragedy and break-up in a home, the same reproachful self-questioning can come to ourselves. We feel that so little on our part, and perhaps on the part of others, could have made such a difference to life – a little more alertness, care, wisdom, sensitivity to feelings that might be hurt, and the death, or the alienation, or the divorce might not have happened! And how human their relationship with him was! They knew him well enough to voice all their self-regrets to him, as the Psalmists so often did in their prayers of complaint to God.

When he heard it from Mary, he wept with her. He understood perfectly how she felt. He appreciated that she found her relief in simply weeping when he was there. When he heard it from Martha with whom he had a quite different relationship, he tried to speak to her the kind of word that he knew would give her hope.

He did not try to apologise to either of them or to give any explanation of why it had all happened. They at least had the comfort of his presence. With him there they were assured more than ever that God himself cared. Martha even as she began speaking to him felt that all was well. *"Even now I know that whatever you ask from God, God will give you."* They could not help trusting him as they had always done. After all, it was a proof of how much he cared, that he had undertaken the journey in face of the threats to his life that had been so recently rumoured. How much he had brought in bringing himself!

Though Jesus shows himself so much one with them, the very conversation which follows Martha's half-sad and half-confident greeting shows how unable they themselves are to be one with him. It is sometimes pointed out that in none of the Gospels do we have any record of Jesus' praying with his disciples. He prays for them, and teaches them to pray, but in his own praying he is shown always alone. In this incident, however, we see him at least expressing the desire for help and fellowship in his own praying, and failing to find it.

What he wanted from them was that they, as well as he himself, might be expectantly prepared for the sign that was to happen, and might pray for it. He was always sensitive to the conditions in which he had to work. Of course he had done mighty works even when the atmosphere around him gave no encouragement and there was no expectation of miracle. But he had often found it helpful and encouraging when people around him had themselves been hopeful and prayerful, and he had been at all times thrilled to find them persistent in their demands and great in their faith. Here at Bethany he knew himself challenged to an effort that was to tax his own faith, expectancy, and self-giving as no other had ever done. He did not want to go to that grave-side entirely isolated and alone in mind and spirit, amongst such a huge crowd of mere on-lookers. He therefore sought to find real support in the fellowship and faith of his two friends. In this case it was Martha he felt he must first approach. It was she who first met him. She was the key person who controlled everything that went on around the home. He knew, too, that he would ultimately need her practical co-operation, for if the stone of the tomb was to be rolled open, it was she who would have to give the order.

He lost no time. When she started the conversation on his arrival he broke in with the news: "*Your brother will rise again.*" The excitement of his voice and the look in his eyes should have helped her to grasp that he meant, "I have come to do it *here and now*"! But there was not a spark of kindled expectancy. She did not even pause to ask him what he meant, but rattled on as if he was merely repeating a dogmatic and pastoral platitude. They had discussed, time and again before, the subject of when the last day might come, and how the dead will all rise. "*I know*", she said, "*that he will rise again in the resurrection at the last day.*"

He made one last effort to switch her mind back from the distant future to the present day, and from dogma to reality. He did it in one of those eloquent and appealing words into which he had the habit of putting so much of himself, a word spoken as if he were addressing not simply the soul there before him, but every coming generation, each with its need to hear the same invitation, and to listen for the same assurance.

"*I am the resurrection and the life;*" he said, "*he who believes in me, though he die, yet shall he live, and whoever lives and believes in me shall never die.*"

He pressed the challenge home: "*Do you believe this?*" He hoped that she would realise now that he had marvellous news to tell her about Lazarus, herself, and her home, here and now. But he found her simply reiterating her agreement with what everyone in his small band of disciples was by now saying about him. "*Yes, Lord; I believe that you are the Christ, the Son of*

God, he who is coming into the world." It certainly was much, but he had wanted much more. He had no opportunity to test Mary herself. She was at the centre of a large crowd of mourners. He gave up trying. It was undoubtedly with disappointment that as so often before, having looked round for human understanding and help, he found it lacking. He had so much to give, and they would take only so little! So far they would go, and no further.

The Sign, the Agony and the Prayer

In the spectacular procession of signs that we have witnessed as we have read through this Gospel, Jesus, there at the centre of everything, has shown himself able to meet whatever form of human need was brought before him, often dramatically majestic, always calm and in control even of the natural world around him. Yet never have we seen him so majestic as he is here. Never has his word been uttered in such a dramatic situation – the large crowd not knowing what is to happen, gathered to watch the tomb opened, the corpse in full view, the command loudly and deliberately given: *"Lazarus, come out."* And it happened: *"The dead man came out, his hands and feet bound with bandages, and his face wrapped with a cloth."* The Word of God has the power to recall into his presence one who has passed through death, to reverse decay and corruption, and to bring the tied-up body out of its tomb.

One striking feature in the Christ who works so marvellously we have not previously in this Gospel been allowed to glimpse. As he approaches the tomb, he is revealed as inwardly engaged in a deep struggle. When he allowed himself to be overcome at the sight of Mary and her friends in tears, we are told that *"he was deeply moved in spirit and troubled"*. We further read that *"deeply moved again, he came to the tomb"*. Commentators often translate these phrases in language more intense in its implications. One translates it that *"he shuddered, moved with the deepest emotion"*. Others mention his *"groaning in spirit"* and *"groaning within himself"*. It is sometimes pointed out that John's Gospel gives us no account of Jesus' agony in the Garden of Gethsemane, and it is suggested that we are meant to think of this agony as the beginning of a long-drawn-out "passion" that came to its full intensity as he went on his way to Calvary.

In the prayer of thanksgiving which he uttered when the stone was removed – *"Father, I thank thee that thou hast heard me"* – it becomes clear that from the moment he knew that he had to raise Lazarus he had been engaged in praying that it might be so. His intercession had been continuous throughout his journey to Bethany and had become more and more intense, finding its expression in his inward agony as the time came closer. Calvin understands the gaze he gave to heaven as a sign of the intensity of his prayer, and as an example to us all: "The fervour of prayer often affects the body in such a way that the body unwittingly follows the mind of its own accord. We certainly cannot doubt that when Christ raised his eyes to heaven he was carried thither with extraordinary vehemence."

As he prayed thus, and as his prayer was being answered he taught us something about the place such prayer had always played in his own life's ministry. *"I knew that thou hearest me always, but I have said this on account of the people standing by, that they may believe that thou didst send me."* Elijah at Carmel drew attention to his prayer and its answer in order to let Israel know that there was a God in Israel and that he himself was his servant (1 Kings 18:36). Jesus here wants his praying to be a public testimony to his own quite unique relationship to God. He wants it known that everything he has accomplished in his ministry on earth has been simply the answer of the Father to his praying – *I knew that thou hearest me always*. Though such praying on his part had never before been revealed with such visible and audible passion, it had always been there as a continuous inner orientation and exercise of mind and heart even during his busiest moments. Calvary itself was now to be his greatest act of prayer, and the Resurrection was to be its final answer.

The Final Word to Martha

It is when we hear Jesus' final word to Martha, that the relevance of the whole incident for our situation today can come most acutely home to us. As Jesus approached the tomb, she demonstrated again her complete inability to understand what he has come to do, and to give him the faith and prayer support he had been seeking. He appealed for her help to have the stone removed, but she resisted and tried to prevent him from going further: *"Lord, by this time there will be an odour, for he has been dead four days."* We can understand her anxiety – always she had been the wise and practical person who could foresee all the difficulties in the venturesome schemes that visionary people sometimes proposed. This one was too much for her. Perhaps, too, what had happened to her poor brother during his last days was so distressing and painful to her that she had been relieved when the stone had been set in place. She may indeed have tried there and then to bury with Lazarus the thoughts of what had been, and of what might have been. The tomb had become in her mind a closed book. She was trying now to write a new chapter and she did not want to go back over it all!

Jesus made a last attempt to overcome her resistance, *"Did I not tell you that if you would believe you would see the glory of God?"* It was certainly a reproach. She had failed to grasp what he had already patiently and clearly told her – how shameful that she should now stand there hindering rather than helping! But it was also an appeal to her. Was he himself not still waiting for her to be with him in heart and spirit? He was praying that even at this late hour she might submit to the inspiration of his own faith and fellowship, begin to share his vision of what was to be, join in the prayers he was making and give him a sign that, even though faintly, she understood something of the cost he was bearing. This final appeal to her was not in vain. Though we are not told how fully she was able there and then to respond in mind and heart, we know that they immediately received orders to remove the stone, and the glory of God was seen.

That he dealt so persistently and patiently with Martha before he finally raised Lazarus can remind us today that he wants especially and personally to deal with us before he begins with our surroundings. We may be very acutely conscious of the great need there is in the human situation around us. Things that are not as they should be in our home life, our Church life, or amongst others we have to deal with from day to day. We have wished and we have prayed that it might be otherwise. We are certain that if only people could be won over to the faith, could learn to trust God and open their situation to him, it would make all the difference. We may have in our praying sent a message to the Lord to come and help us all. Of course he wants to come, and to bring into our personal lives and into the surroundings that we find so depressing and troublesome, everything that he brought into that home at Bethany. But he has got to start somewhere, and we are the first point of contact. He does not want to begin with the Lazarus situation at the tomb, but within ourselves, the key people, like Martha.

He is trying to be thorough with us. We may be sure that he himself has been even more urgently concerned than we have been, about it all. He has been praying more earnestly and decisively for greater things to happen than we ourselves have thought about. He wants us to enter his praying, and indeed his suffering over the situation. He wants us to have his vision of what is meant to happen. Therefore with a measure of both reproach and challenge he says to us today the very same words as he did then to Martha: *"Did I not tell you that if you would believe you would see the glory of God?"* They bring a challenge to us to review in the light of our situation what he has already said to us. Few of us who have already had dealings with him can have escaped hearing the words he is referring to: "Ask, and it will be given you!" "For truly I say to you, if you have faith as a grain of mustard seed, you will say to this mountain, 'Move hence to yonder place', and it will move; and nothing will be impossible to you" (Matt. 7:7, 17:20).

Perhaps he wants us to be more precise and less vague in our praying. He may want our minds to focus on certain definite things we should pray to happen to certain people, knowing that it is here that we find the centre of many of the problems around us. He once suggested that prayer might be seen to be effective when those who prayed could agree to focus on some definite request (cf. Matt. 18:19). Perhaps, also, he wants us to become more urgent in our request and more expectant of an immediate sign that we are heard, and that he is responding. Martha had failed badly in this respect at the beginning of his first interview with her. "*Your brother will rise again,*" he had said, when he told her he had come to raise Lazarus. "Some day it will happen", she had replied, and she had thrown the whole force of his word into the future when he had meant it "here and now".

Might it not be that he is also seeking for himself a more open and deeper entrance into the emotional and psychological problems that might be hindering him from working as freely and fully with us as he would like? We have already raised the suggestion that Martha's resistance to the opening up of the tomb was inspired not only by the fear of the physical "odour" that might embarrass everyone, but also by an unwillingness to have opened up in her mind certain aspects of buried but nagging memory. Whether or not this may be a valid conjecture in the case of Martha, Jesus in seeking to deal with us today may want such a tomb opened. "*Where have you laid him?* – I want to become involved with you at the exact place of your personal hurt and need. Even where the exposure might cause embarrassment both to yourself and others, give me an entrance into where there is any smothered bitterness, or unsolved personal problems so that health and sweetness can be restored, and your commitment to my service can become complete!"

How exactly are we to interpret the promise that we "will see the glory of God"? The whole Gospel has been written to answer this question. In incident after incident, sign after sign, word after word we have been given hints of it. For example we have seen Jesus manifesting the glory of God in saving a critical situation at a simple wedding ceremony, in answering the desperate cry of a father for a dying child, in the sudden transformation of a hopeless and wasted life, in his power to see a group of his own disciples triumphantly through strange and depressing difficulties. He wants our thought of what he can do for us today to be inspired by what we have read of himself in this book. Of course there are differences in how he manifests his glory today and how he did it then. He is not now here in the flesh to repeat the unique and suddenly miraculous signs that then marked him out as the Son of God. We have no need for any more of such signs. He has died, risen, given us the Spirit, and opened up for us a new way of prayer so that different, though even greater works (cf. 14:12) can begin to happen in his name.

It can help us in thinking over the question of what we are to ask of him if we pay heed to what he did say at the tomb: *"Father,"* he prayed *". . . I knew that thou hearest me always."* He himself is the one whose praying is certainly always heard and answered. The praying that arises out of our own wisdom and will is often too foolish and self-centred to be given this kind of status before God. Yet we are given the privilege of uniting with Christ in his own praying. When our prayers are inspired by his Spirit they are echoes of his intercession. Is this not why he went to the length of promising: if you ask anything in my name I will do it? (cf. 14:14). Does this "anything" not mean: whatever he himself has challenged us to ask by his approach, example and inspiration?

Of course he allows us to struggle with our own freedom before him, and warns us constantly to watchfulness and self-examination. The Word of God is not meant to deprive us of sanity and reason. Yet far too many of us in this sphere of our Christian life, tend to bury our talent for fear of making mistakes (Matt. 25:24). We are not open enough to his open invitation and promises. We tend to lay them on the shelf where they will not disturb us, and we content ourselves with the doctrine of prayer that regards it as having only the effect of tuning the mind to whatever must be, because things are as they are.

The Psalmist knew better. Though he always kept in reserve the ultimate hope that in the day when everything on earth collapsed God would then be his "refuge and strength", he nevertheless made sure he prayed to him as a "very present help in trouble" (Ps. 46).